Fli

Preparing for your Flight Review

James D Price
ATP, CFII / MEI

http://www.JDPriceCFI.com

This guide is intended to help pilots prepare for a Flight Review's oral and flight. Should the pilot desire more knowledge, other resources are referenced throughout this study guide.

This publication is printed for informational purposes only, and is not intended to substitute for any approved aircraft flight manual, Flight Service briefing, competent flight instruction, or an official government publication. The navigational charts used herein are not current and should not be used for navigation.

Limitation of Liability

ISBN 978-0-9837506-0-4

Printed in the United States of America
Writers Cramp Publishing
http://www.writerscramp.us

Other books by James D Price

Track Expenses will help you keep
perfect records. You can record
aircraft squawks, and keep track of
maintenance and oil changes.
There's even a spot to record VOR
checks and GPS data updates each
month.

With *Track Expenses Like a PRO,*
you'll always know when
inspections are due, how much your
aircraft costs per year, and you'll be
ready for taxes with business and
charitable deductions.

ISBN 9780977723546

For more information, visit Jim's website at:

http://www.JDPriceCFI.com

Printed in the U.S.A.
http://www.WritersCramp.us

Acknowledgements:

Mooney Aircraft photos, courtesy of Mooney Aircraft Company, Kerrville, TX

Garmin images, courtesy of Garmin, Inc., Olathe, KS

I am grateful to my dear wife Gerry, who encouraged me and helped me find the right words.

Thanks to my friends Phil Corman, Larry Palmer, and Mike McAfee, who liberally donated massive amounts of enthusiasm, and thoughtful, constructive criticism.

I express my eternal gratitude to every pilot that I have flown with, whether as a colleague, student or instructor. I learned something every time I flew with you!

TABLE OF CONTENTS

When my friend, Pete Peterson was asked where he had learned to fly, he replied,
"I soloed in Show Low Arizona in 1935, and I've been learnin' ever since."

2009 Nall Report, Non-Commercial Fixed-Wing Accidents

Type Operation	Accidents	Fatal Accidents	Fatalities
Personal	927 (73%)	186 (77%)	319 (74%)
Instructional	194 (15%)	19 (8%)	31 (7%)

Public use, positioning, aerial observation, business and other working use "type operations", had between a 1 – 4% accident rate.

2009 Nall Report, Light and Weather Conditions: Non-Commercial Fixed Wing

Light/Weather	All Accidents	Fatal Accidents	Lethality
Day VMC	1072 (85%)	160 (68%)	15%
Night VMC	111 (9%)	25 (11%)	23%
Day IMC	41 (3%)	30 (13%)	73%
Night IMC	19 (2%)	15 (6%)	79%
Not reported	11 (1%)	6 (3%)	-

2009 Nall Report, Pilots Involved in Non-Commercial Fixed-Wing Accidents

PIC Certificate Level	Accidents	Fatal Accidents	Lethality
ATP	133 (10%)	28 (12%)	21%
Commercial	339 (27%)	62 (26%)	18%
Private	640 (50%)	126 (52%)	20%
Sport	16 (1%)	1 (<1%)	6%
Student	106 (8%)	7 (3%)	7%
None	23 (2%)	6 (2%)	26%
Unknown	15 (1%)	11 (5%)	73%
Two pilots on board	140 (11%)	32 (13%)	23%
Single pilot CFI	235 (18%	48 (20%)	20%
Single pilot, Instrument-rated	644 (51%)	140 (58%)	22%

Try to learn from the mistakes of others.

You won't live long enough to make all of them by yourself.

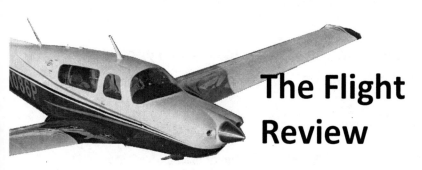

The Flight Review

You need not have a flight review if, within the last two years you:
- ○ Had a flight test for any certificate or rating.
- ○ Had a pilot proficiency check administered by the FAA.
- ○ Had a Part 121 or 135 pilot proficiency check.
- ○ Had a Part 141 Chief pilot proficiency check
- ○ Had a military pilot proficiency check.
- ○ Had a pilot examiner annual flight check.
- ○ Completed any phase of the FAA Wings Program (See *www.FAASafety.gov* for details).

Flight Reviews expire in 24 months on the last day of the 24th month. For instance, if you have a flight review on July 2nd, 2011, it will expire on July 31st, 2013.

Flight Review Facts
- ○ Without a current flight review, you cannot fly as PIC. If you are solo, you're **the PIC**.
- ○ If the flight review is unsatisfactory, the instructor does not document this as a failure.
  - • You may simply correct your deficiencies and either fly again with the same CFI, or take another flight review with a different CFI.
- ○ One Flight Review suffices for <u>all</u> the categories and classes of aircraft that you fly. If you have a flight review in the Goodyear Blimp, you're legal for two more years in your Cessna Citation.
- ○ When the logbook is endorsed by the CFI, indicating that you've passed your flight review, you don't need to carry your logbook with you when you fly. However:
  - • Officials from the FAA, NTSB, and law enforcement, may ask to see your logbook.
  - • An FBO will want to see the Flight Review endorsement, if you wish to rent one of their airplanes.

A Review of Category, Class and Type

Category Examples

Airplane   Rotorcraft   Lighter than air   Glider

Class Examples

Multi Engine Land   Single Engine Land   Single Engine Sea

Type Examples

A type rating is required in a specific make and model of aircraft if:

- o It's powered by one or more turbojet engines (excludes turboprops like the Piper Malibu and smaller / earlier model King Air),

or

- o The aircraft's takeoff gross weight is certified for 12,500 pounds or more (like the larger / later model King Air).

Your Aircraft must have dual flight controls. Why? FAR 61.56 specifies that during a flight review, "flight training" must be given. FAR 91.109 requires flight instruction or training to be given in aircraft with dual controls. Beech Pilot Proficiency Program Flight Reviews in aircraft with a throw over control wheel have an exemption from the dual flight control rule, but the pilot must be PIC. That is, he or she must have a current medical and an unexpired flight review.

Your Certified Flight Instructor (CFI) must be

qualified in your airplane's Category and Class. He or she doesn't need to have five hours of PIC flight time in your aircraft. If you need

a Flight Review in an aircraft that requires a type rating, then your CFI needs to have a type rating in that aircraft.

He or she doesn't need a current FAA Medical if you can be <u>the Pilot In Command (PIC)</u>.

However, if your flight review has expired, your CFI must be the PIC, and will therefore need to have a current medical.

Light Sport Exception

If the aircraft is a light sport, your CFI will need at least five hours of flight time in that make and model Light Sport aircraft.

What to Expect from the Oral and the Flight

The flight review does not involve a written. It requires a <u>minimum</u> of:

- A one hour oral, that **must include** a review of flight rules found in FAR Part 91.
- A one hour flight.

If you are a "15 – 20 hours per year pilot", or you haven't flown for a long time, expect a longer oral and flight.

The Oral

To prepare for the oral, certainly study this book. In addition, you could complete the "*Flight Review Prep Guide*" course available at *www.faasafety.gov*. Bring a copy of the completion certificate to the flight review.

Your CFI <u>may</u> give you a short (no more than 50 nm) cross-country flight plan assignment to an unfamiliar airport. Be sure to consider runway lengths, weather, fuel requirements, terrain, NOTAMs, TRFs, etc. Your CFI <u>could</u> require a manual flight plan, or allow you to prepare using an online planner.

3

The Flight

Your CFI could ask questions to determine your experience and the type of flying that you normally do, and then determine which maneuvers you'll perform. Remember that it's proficiency-based, and the CFI has discretion on how much time and how much instruction is needed to ensure that you are proficient. You must demonstrate that you can <u>safely</u> exercise the privileges of your certificate.

As you fly selected maneuvers, you'll be evaluated on your basic stick and rudder proficiency. As you fly the short cross-country, that's a good place to sample your knowledge of aircraft systems, and your ability to make good decisions when faced with unusual circumstances, (*Aeronautical Decision Making* and *Risk Management*). Your CFI may tell you to consider a mechanical problem or an unexpected weather scenario, which will require a diversion to another airfield.

Use all your tools and resources, including the "Nearest" and "Direct to" functions on your GPS. For more information, see **www.aopa.org/asf/publications/sa03.pdf**

Logging Flight Time

You don't need a current medical to have an annual review, but if your medical has expired, you'll log the time as "dual". Once you get a medical, you can then fly as PIC.

If you have a current medical, then you can log your flight as PIC.

How Much Should You Train?

There are flight departments of all sizes, from the largest airline, to the company that has one plane to run errands. No matter the size, they all want their pilots to be proficient and highly trained. All passengers expect the pilot to be full of knowledge, well trained, proficient, and competent.

Is a Flight Review with a CFI every two years working for you? Perhaps that depends on how much you fly, and how much you feel challenged as an aviator. If you feel that you would like more challenge and training, please go to **www.FAASafety.gov** and register for the Wings program.

Flight Regulations

Preparation Prior to Each Flight
(FAR 91.103)

If you plan to fly outside of the airport area, or file IFR, you must:
- Study weather reports and forecasts.
- Determine fuel requirements.
- Plan alternatives if the planned flight cannot be completed.
- Check with ATC for known traffic delays.
- Determine takeoff and landing distances by evaluating:
  - Runway lengths, elevation and slope.
  - Aircraft gross weight.
  - Wind and temperature.

For Local Flights: You should know about the airport(s) you intend to use. This includes the runway lengths, and takeoff and landing distances for the conditions of the day.

Planning Fuel Requirements

(FAR 91.151 & 167)
- **VFR DAY:** Fuel to destination + 30 minutes.
- **VFR NIGHT:** Fuel to destination + 45 minutes.
- **IFR:** Fuel to destination and alternate + 45 minutes.

"Any attempt to stretch fuel is guaranteed to increase head winds."

According to AOPA's Air Safety Institute, in an average week, three general aviation aircraft crash due to improper fuel management.

Your Responsibility and Authority as the Pilot in Command (PIC) *(FAR 91.3)*

You are directly responsible for, and are the final authority as to the operation of the aircraft.

Deviating From the Rules *(FAR 91.3)*

- o   If an in-flight emergency requires immediate action, the PIC may deviate from any rule necessary to deal with that emergency.
- o   If the PIC deviates from a rule, he or she shall, upon the request of the Administrator, send a written report of that deviation to the Administrator.

PIC Responsibilities *(FAR 91.413)*

The PIC must make sure that his/her aircraft is airworthy. That includes ensuring that:

- o   The aircraft has received an Annual Inspection within the past 12 months. (The annual expires the last day of the 12th month). (FAR 91.409).
- o   The transponder has been tested and inspected within the past 24 months. (Expires the last day of the 24th month).

If you're flying IFR, the Pitot/Static System must have been tested and inspected within the past 24 months. (Expires the last day of the 24th month).

Pilot Preventive Maintenance (CFR Part 43, *Maintenance, Preventative Maintenance, Rebuilding & Alteration)*

Pilots should never exceed their personal skill level when it comes to aircraft maintenance.

A pilot can:

- o   Change the oil and lubricate the wheel bearings.
- o   Refill the hydraulic fluid.
- o   Remove, install, and repair landing gear tires.
- o   Replace the landing gear's elastic shock absorber cords.
- o   Replace defective safety wiring and cotter keys.
- o   Lubricate cover plates, cowlings, and fairings
- o   Add oil or air to landing gear shock struts.

Required Documents in the Aircraft
(FAR 91.203, 91.9)

- o **A**irworthiness certificate.

- o **R**egistration certificate.

- o **R**adio license, (if traveling outside the USA, and for some commercial operations).

- o **O**perating limitations - - (The Owner's Manual).

- o **W**eight and balance data.

Medicals (FAR 61.23)

- o 3rd Class — Good for 60 months, unless you're 40 or over on the day of the examination; then it's good for 24 months.
- o 2nd Class — Good for Commercial privileges the first 12 months. If you don't get another flight physical after 12 months — it turns into a 3rd class physical.
- o 1st Class — ATP privileges during first 6 months, Commercial privileges during the next 6 months. After 12 months — it turns into a 3rd class physical.

There are certain aircraft sounds that can only be heard at night or over large bodies of water.

Flight Physical Expiration Table

(ALL PHYSICALS expire the last day of the month.)

Flight Purpose:	3rd Class	2nd Class		1st Class		
	Personal & Business	Commercial	Personal & Business (3rd Class)	ATP 1st Class	Commercial	Personal & Business (3rd Class)
If you are under 40	60 months	12 months	60 months	12 months	12 months	60 months
If you are 40 or older	24 months	12 months	24 months	6 months	12 months	24 months

REMEMBER, you can submit FAA Form 8500-8 before your physical at: *https://medxpress.faa.gov*
The FAA forwards this information to your Medical Examiner.

Pilot Currency *(FAR 61.56, 61.57)*

Within the preceding 24 calendar months you must have received a Flight Review in **one** of the aircraft in which you're rated.

Landing Currency is Category, Class and Type specific.

*If you'll be carrying passengers **in a particular aircraft**, you'll need, within the past 90 days:*

- o **DAY CURRENCY: Three** takeoffs and landings. (If it's a tail wheel aircraft, those landings need to be to a full stop).
- o **NIGHT CURRENCY**: From one hour after sunset to one hour before sunrise, **three** takeoffs and **three** landings to a **full stop**.

Required Personal Documents *(FAR 61.3)*

When you are flying, you must have with you:
- A current plastic (credit card style) pilot certificate that includes an "English Proficient" endorsement. (Required for international flying).
- An appropriate current medical.
- A photo ID (Driver's license, government ID, military ID, or passport).

Misplaced License

You can request temporary authority to exercise certificate privileges from **www.FAA.gov**. Go to FAA.gov and sign into your account, and click on **Licenses & Certificates**. Next, click on **Airman Online Services**. FAA will send a temporary certificate via fax or e-mail. You can only request one temporary certificate within any six-month period.

While you're there, you can request your **replacement** certificate.

Changed Address and Your Certificate
(FAR 61.60)

The FAA must be notified within **30 days** of an address change, otherwise you may not act as pilot in command. You can change your address, add "English Proficient", or any other amendment to your status by going to **www.FAA.gov,** *and clicking* on the "Licenses & Certificates" TAB.

You may also make changes through the mail, at:

FAA
Airmen Certification Branch,
AFS-760
P.O. Box 25082
Oklahoma City, OK 73125-0082

Required Equipment, VFR
DAY:

- o Fuel gauge for each tank.
- o Oil Temp gauge, (each <u>air cooled</u> engine).
- o Temp gauge, (each <u>liquid cooled</u> engine).
- o Oil Pressure gauge, (each engine).
- o Tachometer, (each engine).
- o Manifold Pressure gauge, for each <u>altitude engine</u>. (That's a turbocharged reciprocating engine. Its manifold pressure is boosted and therefore, one must monitor that pressure).
- o ELT (FAR 91.207).
- o Altimeter.
- o Magnetic Compass.
- o Airspeed Indicator.
- o Landing gear position indicator, (if the aircraft has retractable gear).
- o Seat Belts and shoulder straps, if installed. (Shoulder straps are mandatory if the aircraft was manufactured after July, 1978).

NIGHT:

- o Position lights must be ON from sunset to sunrise. (Ref. FAR 91.209).
- o Anti-Collision light system, (required in small civil airplanes manufactured after March 11, 1996).
  - • If the anti-collision light system fails, you may fly to a place to have it repaired.
- o Landing light, (if flown for hire).
- o A power source, plus spare fuses; 3 of each kind required, and they must be accessible in flight.

Required Equipment for an IFR Flight
(In addition to the equipment required for VFR) *(FAR 91.205)*

- o Clock <u>installed in the aircraft</u>, displaying hours, minutes and seconds.
- o Directional Gyro (DG).
- o Attitude Indicator.
- o Rate of turn indicator & Skid/Slip Indicator.
- o Two-way radios and NAV equipment appropriate to the ground facilities to be used.
- o Altimeter.
- o Generator or Alternator with adequate capacity.

> **NOTE:** You can takeoff with inoperative instruments or equipment that are not required by FAR 91, as long as the "bad" instrument or equipment is removed or placarded *"INOPERATIVE"*, and a pilot or mechanic determines that the loss of that instrument or equipment is not a hazard.

Minimum Equipment List (MEL) *(FAR 91.213)*

An **MEL** can be authorized by the airworthiness certificate holder to allow takeoff with inoperative instruments or equipment. It can never take away from the equipment required for VFR day, VFR night, or IFR (day or night).

- o The MEL must be approved by the FAA.
- o The MEL and the FAA's letter of approval must be carried in the aircraft.

Stations, Seatbelts, and Shoulder Harnesses
(FAR 91.107)

As pilot in command, you'll need to ensure that each passenger has been:

- o Briefed on how to fasten and unfasten their safety belt, and if applicable, their shoulder harness*.
- o Notified to fasten his/her safety belt/shoulder harness* before aircraft movement.

Passengers must be in an **appropriate seat with their safety belt/shoulder harness fastened during taxi, takeoff and landing.

*Shoulder straps must be installed if the aircraft was manufactured after July, 1978.
**If a child is less than 24 months old, he or she can be held on a passenger's lap.
See FAR 91.107 for child approved seat/restraint systems.

Minimum Safe Altitudes (FAR 91.119)

Anywhere – Fly at an altitude that will allow a safe emergency landing without hazard to people or property on the surface.

1,000'

Congested Areas: Fly no closer than **1,000 feet** above the highest obstacle within **2,000 feet** of the aircraft.

500'

Other than congested areas and over water and sparsely populated areas: Fly no closer than **500 feet** to any person, vessel, vehicle or structure.

Acrobatic Flight (FAR 91.303)

You cannot perform acrobatics:
- o Over a congested area or settlement.
- o Over an open air assembly.
- o Within Class B, C, D, or Class E <u>if it's designated for an airport.</u>
- o Within 4 nm of a federal airway (Class E).
- o Below 1,500 feet AGL.
- o When visibility is less than 3 statute miles.

Acrobatic Flight Defined

Acrobatic flight means an intentional maneuver involving an abrupt change in the aircraft's attitude, an abnormal attitude, or abnormal acceleration that is not necessary for flight. It also means:
- o Exceeding 60° of bank.
- o Exceeding 30° pitch – nose up or nose down.

Acrobatic Flight and Parachutes (FAR 91.307)

Unless each occupant is wearing a parachute, no pilot carrying any person (other than a crew member) may execute acrobatic maneuvers.

This does not apply to spins or other flight maneuvers required by the regulations for a certificate or rating, when given by a CFI, etc.

Formation Flying *(FAR 91.111)*

It's never done:
- ○ Without prior arrangement with the pilots of all aircraft involved.
- ○ If carrying passengers for hire.

Cruising Altitudes *(FAR 91.179)*

GREATER THAN 3,000 FEET AGL, BUT LESS THEN 18,000 FEET MSL, FLY:

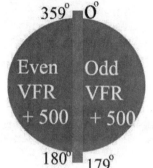

359° 0°

Even VFR + 500

Odd VFR + 500

180° 179°

Choosing an appropriate altitude is based on magnetic degrees <u>track</u>, not magnetic degrees heading.

Order of Right of Way *(FAR 91.113)*

BALLOON has the right of way over everything.

GLIDER — It's the next least Maneuverable and has the right of way over an airplane or a rotorcraft.

AIRCRAFT TOWING OR REFUELING another aircraft have the right of way over all other engine driven aircraft.

AIRCRAFT IN DISTRESS have the right-of-way over <u>all</u> other aircraft.

Converging, Approaching Head-On, and Overtaking *(FAR 91.111)*

- o **IF CONVERGING** — an aircraft on the right has the right of way, (if it's the same category aircraft).
- o **IF APPROACHING HEAD-ON** — both aircraft should alter course to the right.
- o **IF OVERTAKING** — the overtaken aircraft has the right of way. The pilot of the overtaking aircraft alters course to the right.

Right of Way While Landing *(FAR 91.113)*

- o Final approach or landing aircraft have the right of way.
  - • If you're at a lower altitude, you have the right of way, but you should never take advantage of your position.

Oxygen *(FAR 91.211)*

ABOVE 15,000 MSL:	Oxygen available for everyone.
ABOVE 14,000 MSL:	Oxygen is required for flight crew at all times.
14,000 MSL ⇧ 12,500 MSL ⇩	Oxygen is required for flight crew after 30 minutes.

Supplemental oxygen can help prevent hypoxia symptoms when flying:

- o At or above 5,000 feet MSL at night.
- o At or above 10,000 feet MSL during the day

ELTs

An ELT must be attached to the airplane and the ELT batteries must be checked annually for corrosion.

The ELT batteries must be replaced:

- o If the transmitter has been in use for more than 1 cumulative hour,

or

- o When either 50% of their useful life, *or* 50% of their charge life has expired.

406 MHz ELTs

On **February 1, 2009,** the international COSPAS-SARSAT satellite system discontinued satellite-based monitoring of the 121.5 and 243 MHz frequencies.

121.5 / 243 MHz distress signals are now, only detected by local airport facilities, air traffic control facilities, or by overflying aircraft. This assumes that an overflying aircraft will be monitoring 121.5. If an aircraft crashes, especially in a remote area, a **121.5 MHz ELT** will provide extremely limited assistance.

The new **406 MHz ELTs** are monitored by satellites and also contain a 121.5 MHZ ELT. Optionally, they can be linked to a GPS, to provide precise coordinates to search responders.

If you don't have a 406 ELT, consider carrying a personal locator beacon, (PLB).

It's your choice. Base your decision on the type of flying you do, the equipment you carry, and the type of terrain you overfly.

"In flying I have learned that carelessness and overconfidence are usually far more dangerous than deliberately accepted risks".
Wilbur Wright in a letter to his father, September 1900

(Photo – Ohio Historical Society)

"Rules are made for people who aren't willing to make up their own."
Chuck Yeager

Judgment Creep

If a pilot pushes a limit, and gets away with it, his or her judgment creeps to the "Edge", setting a new, bolder limit. Creeping closer and closer to the edge of the safety envelope will eventually result in a Judgment Spiral.

Aeromedical Concerns

Drugs and Alcohol (FAR 91.17)

You can't be a crew member if:

- o You're using any drug that effects your physical or mental capacities in any way.
- o You've consumed alcohol within eight hours.
  - You could be under the influence after 8 hours. Therefore, you would be wise to allow **12 to 24** hours from bottle to throttle.

You're under the influence if your blood alcohol **is .04% or more**.

Passengers & Substance Abuse

If your passenger(s) cannot correctly pronounce "innovative", "preliminary", "proliferation", or "cinnamon" – they may be under the influence. So, except in an emergency, a pilot may not allow anyone to board his/her aircraft if they appear to be intoxicated or under the influence of drugs. The exception is a medical patient under proper care.

Consider This:

Drunk passengers aboard a short charter flight off Canada's West Coast, likely caused the crash of a float-equipped Cessna 185 in May 2010. A rear-seat passenger pushed the pilot's seat forward with his or her feet and held him and the control

column pinned to the panel. The chartered aircraft dove at a 45° angle into the ocean off Ahousat, an isolated community on the west coast of Vancouver Island. The pilot could have refused the charter if he thought the passengers might be drunk enough to be a safety hazard. This decision cost him his life.

Refusing to Submit to a Drug or Alcohol Test *(FAR 61.14)*
That's grounds for denying an application for any certificate or rating for a year, and suspension or revocation of any certificate or rating.

Carbon Monoxide is a big concern, especially in the winter. Most heaters work by air flowing over the manifold. If exhaust fumes escape, the results could be fatal. If you detect the odor of exhaust or feel drowsy, dizzy, or have a headache while using the heater, you should suspect carbon monoxide poisoning.

"Airplanes are near perfect. All they lack is the ability to forgive."
Richard Collins, Aviation Author

Airspace

AN OPERATING MODE C is required in Class A, Class B, (within 30 nm of the Class B's primary airport), in <u>and above</u> Class C, and when operating above 10,000 MSL, (excluding airspace below 2,500 AGL).

Class A

| Flight Level 600 |
| 18,000' MSL |

Starts above 18,000' MSL and Altimeters must be set to 29.92.
In Class A, you must be on an IFR flight plan with an ATC clearance. (No VFR or VFR on Top in Class A).
Above FL600, it's Class E airspace
Class A exists in all the lower 48 states, and all but the western portion of Alaska.

Class B

Class B airspace surrounds busy airports, like Los Angeles, Chicago O'Hare, Phoenix, Detroit, etc.

CERTIFICATE & TRAINING REQUIREMENTS: Pilots only need a Private Pilot certificate to operate in Class B.
Student Pilots can fly in Class B, but they must have received Class B ground and flight instruction. Student Pilots must have a Logbook endorsement to operate within a specific Class B, and it must be endorsed by the instructor who provided the instruction within the last 90 days. The endorsement can authorize takeoffs and landings at a specific airport in Class B airspace.
Recreation Pilots may fly in Class B airspace if they have an endorsement for ATC communications.

Very busy CLASS B PRIMARY AIRPORTS like Chicago O'Hare (ORD) and Los Angeles (LAX) may exclude student takeoffs and landings.

TO ENTER VFR, one must hear the controller say, "Cleared into class B".

> **CLASS B VFR WEATHER REQUIREMENTS:** 3 miles visibility and clear of clouds.

You'll need mode C inside the 30 nm mode C veil. This veil is a 30 mile ring surrounding the primary airport.

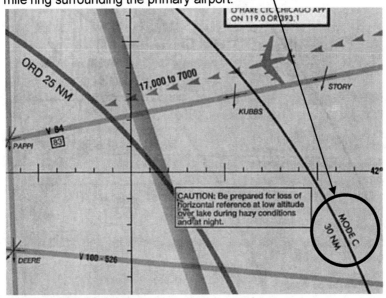

No transponder? No problem. You can request permission to fly in Class B one hour prior to the desired operation.

CLASS B STRUCTURE: It's shaped like an upside down, multi-level wedding cake, with the middle layer starting at the ground and extending up. How high? It varies from 7,000 feet MSL at some coastal airports, to 12,000 feet MSL at Denver. The average is 10,000 feet MSL. Check the chart.

Class B airspace is depicted on WACs, Sectionals and TACs by dark blue lines.

Sectors further away from the primary airport depict different bases.

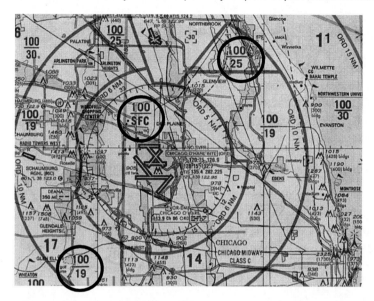

TRAFFIC SEPARATION SERVICE:
VFR aircraft are separated from all aircraft in Class B with traffic advisories.

SPECIAL VFR:
Some Class B airspaces prohibit Special VFR flights.

SPEED LIMITS:
- o Maximum 200 knots for aircraft flying beneath Class B airspace.
- o Maximum 250 knots for aircraft flying within class B airspace. (FAR 91.117)

FAASafety.gov offers an online course: "*A Direct Approach to Class B VFR Operations*"

Class C

CERTIFICATE REQUIREMENTS: Pilots need at least a Student Pilot Certificate.

TO ENTER VFR: Mode C is required in <u>and above</u> Class C airspace.  Establish contact with ATC, with the controller acknowledging you **by call sign**. For instance, "Cessna 7462Q, standby," is an acknowledgement. "Aircraft calling Tucson approach, standby," is NOT an acknowledgement!

The words, "Cleared to enter Class C airspace" <u>are not</u> required.

CLASS C VFR WEATHER REQUIREMENTS: 3 miles visibility. Cloud clearance: 500 feet below, 1000 feet above, and 2,000 feet horizontally.

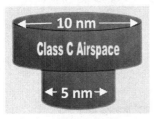

CLASS C STRUCTURE: The core surface area has a **radius of five nautical miles** and extends from the surface to the ceiling of the Class C airspace. The upper "shelf" area has a **radius of ten nm** and extends from as low as 1,200 feet up to the ceiling of the airspace. (AIM 3-2-4).

An outer area, (20 nm radius), is not depicted and it's not part of Class C. However, participating VFR aircraft in that area will receive Class C service from ATC. This is a good place to initiate contact with approach control.

Class C is depicted on WACs and Sectionals by dark magenta lines. Some TACs include Class C airspace. For instance, on the Chicago TAC, the Midway Class C exists below the Chicago O'Hare Class B airspace.

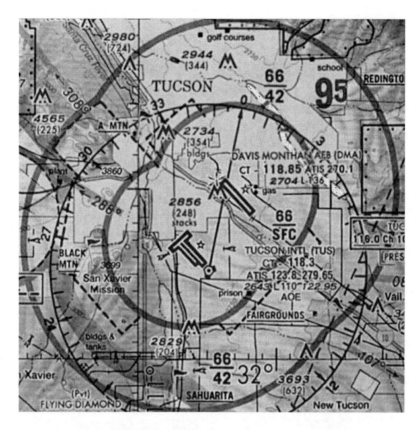

TRAFFIC SEPARATION SERVICE:
VFR aircraft are separated from IFR aircraft in Class C with traffic advisories.

SPECIAL VFR:
Special VFR flights are allowed.

SPEED LIMIT:
Max 200 knots at and below 2,500 AGL & within 4 nm. (FAR 91.117)

23

Class D

CERTIFICATE REQUIREMENTS: Pilots need at least a Student Pilot Certificate.

TO ENTER: Two-way communication with ATC must be established. A transponder is NOT required.

When the tower is closed, Class D airspace becomes Class E or class G. Check the AF/D for actual airspace reversion.

CLASS D STRUCTURE: Class D airspace is generally circular in form and normally extends from the surface to 2,500 feet above the ground. The outer radius of the airspace is variable, but is generally 5 statute miles.

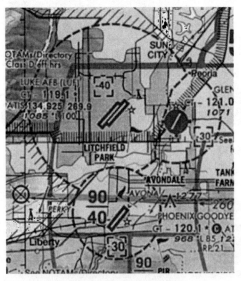

Class D is depicted on Sectional and TAC charts by blue dashed lines.

"-30" Indicates that Class D extends up to **but not including** 3,000 MSL. This is usually the case with a Class D that underlies Class B airspace.

"39" indicates that Class D extends to and including 3,900 feet MSL.

Class D VFR weather requirements: 3 miles visibility. Cloud clearance: 500 feet below, 1000 feet above, and 2,000 feet horizontally.

SPEED LIMIT:
Max 200 knots at and below 2,500 AGL & 4 nm. *(FAR 91.117)*

SPECIAL VFR:
Generally, Special VFR is allowed in Class D, day or night . . .
unless otherwise depicted by "NO SVFR" on the chart.

When an airport name has a box around it, it means that more
information is available in the A/FD.

Class E

There are no minimum equipment requirements in Class E.
Class E is depicted on the Sectional Chart and extends to 18,000
feet MSL, where it meets Class A. airspace.

Class E starts at 700 feet AGL, when it's depicted by a magenta-
tinted vignette, (continues to 18,000 feet MSL). The hard edge is
the extent of Class E where it abuts Class G airspace.

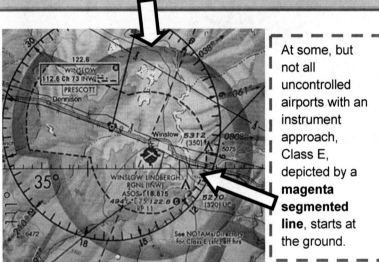

At some, but not all uncontrolled airports with an instrument approach, Class E, depicted by a **magenta segmented line**, starts at the ground.

Magenta Class E areas are used to transition between the terminal
and en-route environments around non-towered airports.

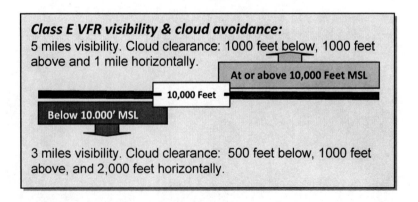

Class E VFR visibility & cloud avoidance:
5 miles visibility. Cloud clearance: 1000 feet below, 1000 feet
above and 1 mile horizontally.

At or above 10,000 Feet MSL

10,000 Feet

Below 10.000′ MSL

3 miles visibility. Cloud clearance: 500 feet below, 1000 feet
above, and 2,000 feet horizontally.

Class E starts at 1,200 feet AGL when it's depicted by a blue-tinted vignette, (continues to 18,000 feet MSL). The hard edge is the extent of Class E where it abuts Class G airspace.

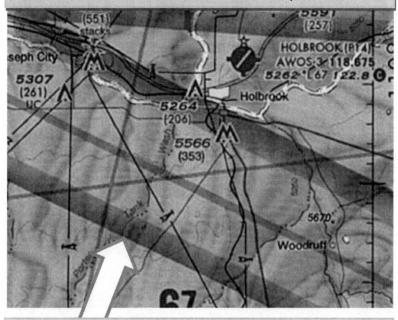

This Class E, depicted in blue, is shown around a Victor airway. (Basically, four nm either side.)

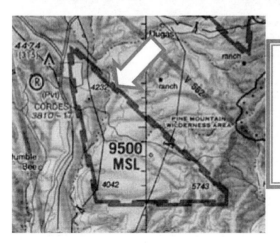

Blue jagged lines differentiate Class E Airspace that starts higher than 1,200 feet AGL. In this case, it starts at 9,500 feet MSL.

Class G

Class G airspace includes all airspace not otherwise classified as controlled below flight level 600. (AIM 3-3-1) There are no entry or clearance requirements for Class G airspace. Class G airspace is typically the airspace very near the ground (1200 feet or less), beneath Class E airspace. When it abuts Class E, Class G is outside of the hard edge of Class E's blue-tinted or magenta tinted vignettes. The floor of Class E is the top of Class G.

Radio communication is not required in Class G airspace, even for IFR operations. Class G is completely uncontrolled, yet it has the most complicated visibility and cloud avoidance rules.

Class G visibility & cloud avoidance:
CLOUD CLEARANCE - 500 feet below, 1000 feet above and 2,000 feet horizontally
DAY – 1 mile visibility. **NIGHT** – 3 miles visibility .

More than 1200 feet AGL, but Less than 10000 MSL

1200 feet or less AGL

NIGHT – 3 miles visibility & 500 feet below, 1000 feet above, and 2,000 feet horizontally.

AOPA's online course, "Know Before You Go: Navigating Today's Airspace", is available at AOPA.org

Terminal Radar Service Area (TRSA)

TRSAs are situated over some selected airports. Participation is VOLUNTARY.

TRSAs are depicted on **sectional charts** by solid **DARK GRAY** lines (see arrows below) and groups of numbers representing the vertical dimensions of the TRSA in hundreds of feet MSL.

Palm Springs Intl. (PSP), in this example, shows the standard depiction of class D airspace (dashed blue lines surrounding PSP), accompanied by solid black lines representing the TRSA dimensions. The portion of TRSA extending outside the PSP surface area is delegated to radar approach control.

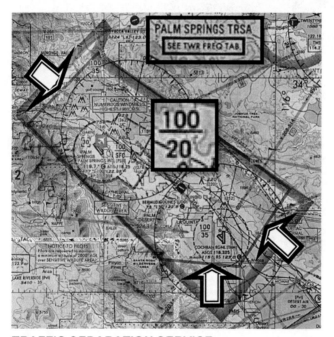

TRAFFIC SEPARATION SERVICE:

A TRSA provides VFR aircraft traffic advisories and separation by ATC.

Arriving VFR aircraft receiving TRSA services will be handed off to tower from approach control.

Departing VFR aircraft are assumed to want TRSA service unless the pilot states, "Negative TRSA service," or a similar comment.

Special VFR

It's allowed in Class C, D, E, and some Class B airspace below 10,000 feet MSL within the airspace contained by the upward extension of the lateral boundaries of the controlled airspace designated to the surface for an airport. That is, if the airspace is in

the shape of a wedding cake, it's allowed only within the inner / surface core. Requires 1 mile visibility and you must remain clear of clouds.

Special VFR requires a clearance from an instrument controller, usually arranged through the airport's tower.

You need to be in contact with a controller who can advise you about, and keep you separated from the IFR traffic that's flying through the clouds – the very same clouds that you'll be dodging.

Don't expect a Special VFR Clearance at a very busy airport. Many class B airports specify "No special VFR" on the chart.

Smart pilots would never try this at night, although it's legal for instrument rated pilots if they're flying an instrument capable aircraft.

1 mile visibility

Clear of clouds

+

Clearance from an "instrument controller"

Special Use Airspace – Military and TFRs

Prohibited Airspace – Never violate it.

It has been established for security or other reasons associated with the national welfare.

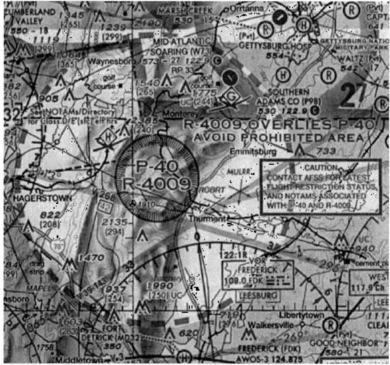

Check the Sectional, TAC or WAC "Frequency Panel" for altitudes affected, time of use, controlling agency and frequency.

Check NOTAMS

Prohibited airspace can grow. For example: P-40, over Camp David, MD, expands (by NOTAM) from a 6 nm radius to 20 nm, (if the President is there).

Violating prohibited airspace may result in military interception and/or the possibility of an attack upon the violating aircraft. Aircraft violating or about to violate prohibited airspace will often be warned beforehand on 121.5 MHz.

Restricted Airspace

Restricted areas denote the existence of unusual, often invisible hazards to aircraft such as artillery firing, aerial gunnery, or guided missiles. Penetration of restricted areas without authorization from the using or controlling agency may be extremely hazardous to the aircraft and its occupants.

Restricted Airspace is depicted by dark blue lines with thin blue lines perpendicular to the outer boundary line.

ATC will allow aircraft to operate in the restricted airspace if the restricted area is not active and it has been released to the controlling agency.

Check the Sectional, TAC or WAC front or back panel for altitudes affected, time of use, controlling agency and frequency.

| R-2510A | TO 15,000 | 0700-2300 †24 HRS IN ADVN | LOS ANGELES CNTR | 128.6 |

In the Frequency Panel example above, R-2310A can be active with 24 hours notice. Always check with the controlling agency before flying in a Restricted Area, even if you believe it is NOT ACTIVE.

Warning Area

This airspace extends from three nautical miles outward from the coast of the U.S. Because Warning areas are over international waters, they cannot be designated a Restricted Area. Nevertheless, they contain activity that may be hazardous to nonparticipating aircraft.

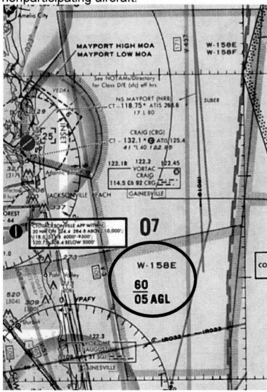

Check the Sectional, TAC or WAC "Frequency Panel" for altitudes affected, time of use, controlling agency and frequency.

Military Operating Area (MOA)

MOAs separate military training activities from IFR traffic.

Pilots operating VFR should exercise extreme caution while flying within a MOA. Contact any FSS within 100 miles of the area to obtain the MOA's hours of operation.

Check the Sectional, TAC or WAC front or back panel for altitudes affected, time of use, controlling agency and frequency.

MOA NAME	ALTITUDE*	TIME OF USE†	CONTROLLING AGENCY/ CONTACT FACILITY	FREQUENCIES
AUSTIN 1	200 AGL	0800-2100 MON-FRI	OAKLAND CNTR	128.8 285.5
			SALT LAKE CITY CNTR	132.25 338.35

Prior to entering an active MOA, contact the controlling agency for traffic advisories.

MOA's are depicted on Sectional, VFR Terminal Area, and Enroute Low Altitude charts.

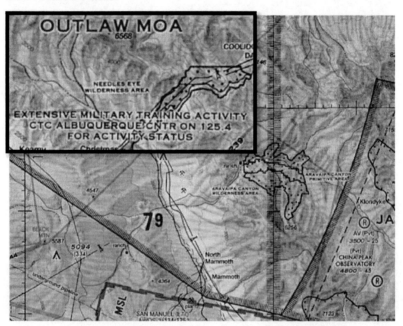

Alert Areas contain a high volume of pilot training or an unusual type of aerial activity. Pilots of participating aircraft as well as pilots transiting the area are **equally responsible** for collision avoidance.

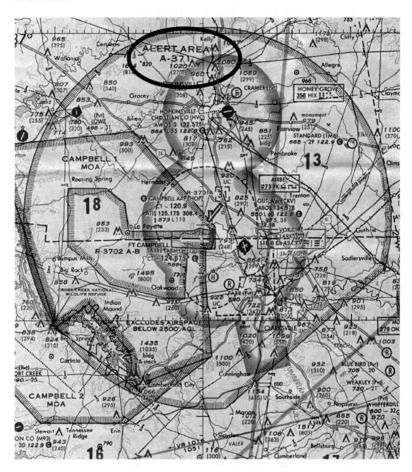

Special Air Traffic Rule (SATR)

In the Phoenix, AZ area, a SATR has been inserted into Luke AFB's Alert Area. While contacting ATC in an Alert Area is usually voluntary, the Luke AFB SATR **requires** all pilots to contact Luke Approach Control.

Controlled Firing Area (CFA)

Controlled firing area activities are suspended immediately when spotter aircraft, radar, or ground lookout positions indicate an aircraft might be approaching the area. There is no need to chart CFA's since they do not cause a nonparticipating aircraft to change its flight path. CFA locations can be located in the A/FD's "Special Notices" section.

Military Training Routes

Military aircraft operating below 10,000 feet, sometimes faster than 250 knots.

Military Training Routes are divided into Instrument Routes (**IR**), and Visual Routes (**VR**).

IR routes are flown under Air Traffic control, while VR routes are not.

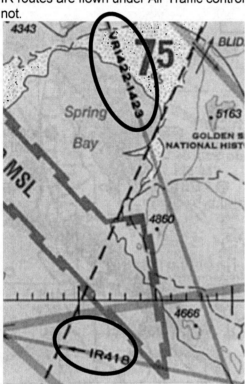

Each route is identified by either IR or VR, followed by either:

- o *Four digits for routes below 1,500 feet AGL, such as: VR1422.*
- o *Three digits for routes with at least one leg above 1,500 ft AGL, such as: IR418.*

An arrow by an IR or VR route designation indicates the direction of flight on the route.

Special Flight Rules Area (SFRA) is a region in which the normal regulations of flight do not apply, especially those concerning airspace classification, altitude, course, and speed restrictions, etc.

SFRAs are over the Grand Canyon, Ketchikan, AK, Valparaiso, FL, New York City Class B airspace, and the Washington, D.C. metropolitan area. There are also SFRAs within Los Angeles International Airport Class B airspace, Anchorage International Airport, and Elmendorf AFB Class C airspace.

Flying into the Washington D.C. SFRA requires special training, available at FAASafety.gov. Log in and search the "Course Catalogue" for **ALC-55: Washington DC Special Flight Rules Area (SFRA).** After you complete the training, print the certificate of achievement, and keep it with you. You may be required to show it to an official.

AOPA's online course, "Mission Impossible – Navigating Today's Special-Use Airspace", is available at AOPA.org.

Temporary Flight Restriction (TFR)

Check **http://TFR.FAA.gov** for active TFRs, which are displayed with the FDC NOTAMS. For the latest information, you should call your local Flight Service Station at 1-800-WX-BRIEF.

Disaster and Fire TFRs:

- o Protect persons and property in the air and on the surface.
- o Provide a safe environment for the operation of disaster relief aircraft.
- o Prevent the unsafe congestion of sightseeing aircraft above an incident or event.

Stadium and Racetrack TFRs:

- o When an event is occurring, avoid these by **3,000 feet AGL and 3 nm**.
- o FAA does will not remind you about sporting events.
- o It's a "Blanket NOTAM"; always there.

Presidential TFRs:

- o These are airspace bubbles around the President, Vice President, and other public officials.
- o Very secret, so <u>no</u> advanced notice is required.
- o It's your responsibility to know the TFR is there.
- o The TFR could involve several airports.

Missile Launch TFRs:

- o These TFRs protect aircraft and space crews.

Other TFRs

Laser demonstrations, power plants, (nuclear, hydro-electric, and coal), dams, refineries, industrial complexes, military facilities, etc.
Pilots should avoid these areas. Never loiter above them.

Go to http://SUA.FAA.gov for a Special Use Airspace map **and** http://tfr.faa.gov for TFRs.

Go to www.SeeAndAvoid.org for the real time status of military airspace; actual and near mid-air locations.

AERONAUTICAL CHARTS

Always fly with a current chart.

The Airport Facility Directory (A/FD) contains **Aeronautical Chart Bulletins** and changes to current charts.

FAA NOTAMS also contain changes that may have occurred since a CURRENT chart was published.

The A/FD is available FREE online at www.faa.gov (or perform an online search for "Airport Facility Directory").

World Aeronautical Charts (WAC)

Revised annually, WACs are designed for moderate speed aircraft and visual navigation. Some Alaskan, Mexican, and Caribbean WACs are revised every two years.

Sectional Charts

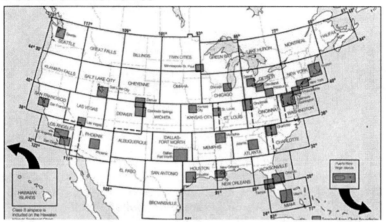

Revised every six months, Sectionals are designed for slow or medium speed aircraft and visual navigation. They're named after a major city on the chart.

Terminal Area Chart (TAC)

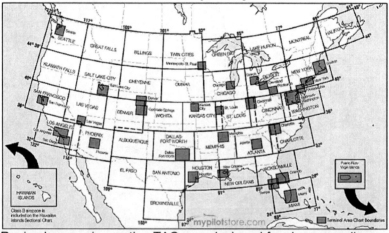

Revised every six months, TACs are designed for slow or medium speed aircraft and visual navigation. The TAC has greater detail and is perfect for use in congested areas.

The TAC's VFR Flyway Planning Chart depicts flight paths to help you remain clear of busy traffic.

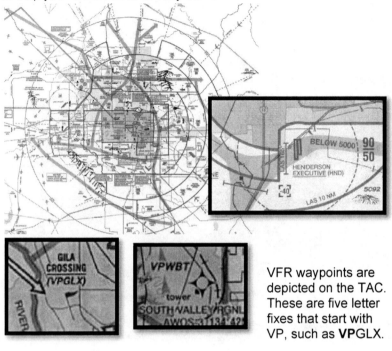

VFR waypoints are depicted on the TAC. These are five letter fixes that start with VP, such as **VP**GLX.

These waypoints are depicted by either a magenta flag symbol or a black waypoint star symbol.

Correcting for Magnetic Variation

Measure the TRUE heading, and using the magnetic variation shown on the chart:

- o Add a West variation to the true heading for a MAG Heading
- o Subtract an East variation from the true heading for a MAG Heading.

East is least

West is best

41

Chart Quiz

Questions: On the below Phoenix Sectional, Chandler (CHD) has a part time tower. (1) This is indicated by _____. The tower uses two frequencies. (2) The frequency _____ is used for CTAF when the tower is closed.
(3) The _____ indicates CTAF. (4) Do you fly a Left or Right pattern for runway 4L?

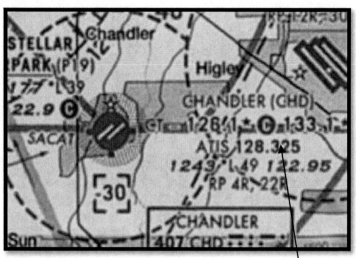

Answers:
(1) The star ★
(2) 126.1 – the frequency to the left of the circled C is the CTAF.
(3) Circled C
(4) Left. 4R and 22R use a right pattern.

The WAC Chart covering the same area does not indicate the after-hours CTAF frequency, the UNICOM frequency, nor the non-standard pattern directions.

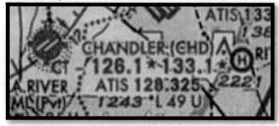

NOTAMs

30 June 2011, the NOTAM system changed to an ICAO standard.

Distant (D) NOTAMs include:

- o Time critical information that may affect safety such as:
  - Airport closure or
  - Inoperative navigational facility.
- o Key words within the first part of the text specifying what the NOTAM concerns. For instance:
  - RWY (Runway)
  - TWY (Taxiway)
  - SVC (Services

D NOTAM examples:

LAX NAV RWY 24R ILS OTS WEF 1106132100-1106132300

LAX TWY C CLSD BTN TWY P,C12 WEF 1106111400-1106131400

CDC 01/044 DXZ RWY 19 MALSR CMSN

FDC NOTAMS (Flight Data Center) are regulatory and include:

- o Standard instrument departures (SIDs),
- o Graphic obstacle clearance departures (ODPs) and
- o Standard terminal arrivals (STARs)
- o Airspace usage.
- o TFRs and permanently closed airports.

FDC NOTAM examples:

FDC **1/8276** (KLAX A0858/11) LAX FI/T LOS ANGELES INTL, LOS ANGELES, CA. ILS OR LOC RWY 6R, AMDT 17... S-ILS 6R DA 580/HAT 472 ALL CATS. VISIBILITY CAT A/B 2400, CAT C/D 5000 S-LOC 6R MDA 580/HAT 472 ALL CATS. SIDESTEP RWY 6L 580/HAT 472 ALL CATS. VDP 1.24 NM TO RW6R TEMPORARY CRANE 446 MSL 1.2 NM SOUTHEAST OF RWY 6R

UAR – indicates a change to a departure procedure (DP) or SID

UAR **12/013** (KPHX A1411/10) PHX AIRSPACE KOOLY3 ARRIVAL (RNAV) RUNWAY 25L TRANSITION PROCEDURE FROM GIPSE TO SCADE UNUSBL. EXPECT RADAR VECTORS AFTER GIPSE. LOST COMMUNICATIONS: AT GIPSE INTERCEPT AND EXECUTE RUNWAY 25L ILS APCH, IF UNABLE PROCEED DIRECT PXR VORTAC AND HOLD, MAINTAIN 9000.

USD – indicates a change to an arrival (STAR)

USD **08/160** (KPHX A0897/10) PHX AIRSPACE CHEZZ TWO DEPARTURE (RNAV): ALL TRANSITIONS NA EXCEPT DRYHT TRANSITION. ADD NOTE: DME/DME/IRU OR GPS REQUIRED.

The FAA posts NOTAMS at
www.faa.gov/pilots/flt_plan/notams/

"An aircraft may disappoint a good pilot, but it won't surprise him or her."
Len Morgan

AIRPORT OPERATIONS

Taxiway and Runway Ops
Airport Signage
Displaced Thresholds/EMAS
Airport Lighting
Traffic Patterns

Taxiway and Runway Operations

Taxi To . . .

ATC Ground Controllers are required to provide explicit taxi instructions to cross or hold short of each runway that intersects the taxi route . . . ("Cessna XYZ, taxi to runway 21 Left via Alpha and Lima. Cross runway 05, hold short of Runway 21 Right.")

Land and Hold Short Operations (LAHSO)

Requires ceiling and visibility of 1000 & 3 (AIM 4-3-11)

- ○ ATC may clear a pilot to land and hold short, and if the PIC believes there's enough available landing distance (ALD), he or she can accept a LAHSO clearance.
- ○ ALD data is contained in the special notices section of the Airport/Facility Directory (A/FD). Controllers will also provide ALD data upon request.
- ○ Student pilots and pilots not familiar with the airport should not accept "Land and Hold Short" clearances.

Safe Taxi Tips

Before You Taxi for Takeoff:

- ○ Study the airport diagram, noting potential hot spots and areas of confusion.
- ○ Plan your taxi using the airport diagram.
- ○ When ATC provides taxi instructions, don't rely on your memory. Write it down.
- ○ Focus on ATC's instructions, and not on how you may have done it a thousand times before. This time it might be different.

- Resolve questions about your clearance with ATC before you move your aircraft. If you're taxiing, stop! It's much easier to ask ATC now, than to explain yourself later.
- Program the flight navigational and communication equipment on the ramp prior to taxi, or while in the run up area – never while the aircraft is in motion.

Taxiing for Takeoff

- Keep a mental map of other traffic.
- All taxi operations are VFR – A "see and avoid" operation.
- Observe a sterile cockpit while taxiing. Keep your conversation professional and operationally focused.
- Always monitor the assigned frequency.
- When you're on the runway, holding in position, the controller will advise you of other aircraft that are on final for your runway, or those that are taking off or landing on intersecting runways. Mentally map other aircraft and their positions.
- When cleared to "line up and wait", note the time. If the tower controller has not cleared you for takeoff in 30 seconds, ask the controller, "How much longer?" (The controller may have forgotten you).
- Verify compass headings, comparing them to taxiways and to the assigned runway. This will help ensure that you don't wander onto the wrong taxiway, or take off on the wrong runway.
- At night, use the edge lighting to distinguish between taxiways and runways.

> **Always read back "hold short" instructions**

For a chilling video of what can happen when pilots and controllers are confused, take a look the videos at **www.airboyd.tv** and in the search box at the bottom of the web page, enter "Providence". There are two videos.

Runways 2/20 & 13/31

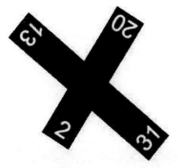

These runways make it easy to transpose the numbers. Take extra care.

"Cleared to Cross" - Not so fast!

When ATC gives you a crossing clearance, read back the clearance, and then wait a few seconds. If the controller does not change his/her mind, (retracting the clearance), then start your taxi. This technique gives the controller a "fighting chance" to stop you if you misunderstood a clearance, answered for another aircraft, or if the controller made a mistake.

"Read back- Hear back" is a method used by pilots and ATC. When the pilot reads back the clearance and the controller hears back the response, he or she is checking for the correct pilot understanding.

Before You Land

- o Review the airport diagram, noting potential hot spots and areas of confusion.
- o An early landing clearance is cause for alert. The controller might forget you and focus on other aircraft.
- O *Plan your taxi using the airport diagram, asking yourself:*
  - • What runway exit will I probably use?
  - • What's my goal? Left or right to the FBO, fuel pumps, hangar, or tie downs?
  - • Are there runways that I'll need to <u>not cross</u> without clearance?

After Landing

- o Clear the runway's protected area, ensuring your entire aircraft is beyond the runway hold line and then stop your aircraft.
- o Obtain taxi clearance before proceeding.

Airport Signage

Location Sign: *"Yellow on black. It's where you're at."*

(White on red)

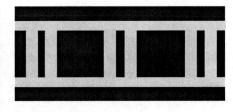

(Yellow on black)

ILS Hold Sign and its associated Taxiway Markings: Hold here when instructed by ATC, because approaches are being conducted with ceilings and visibility less than 800' and 2. Taxiing beyond the taxiway markings can interfere with aircraft on the ILS approach.

Edge of the Runway's Protected Area Marking: *(Yellow on black).*

"Stop solidly at the solid lines."

"Dash across the dashed lines."

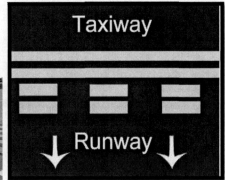

Enhanced Centerline

Yellow dashes placed on both sides of the taxiway centerline within 150 feet of the runway hold-short line. This alerts pilots that they are approaching a runway holding position.

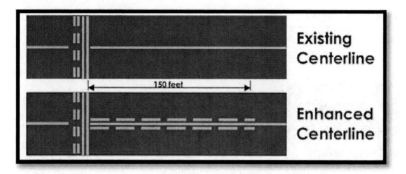

Edge of the Non-Movement Area (Ramp) and Taxiways
Marking (Controlled): (Yellow on black)
STOP and get a clearance before you taxi beyond the solid line.

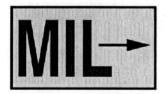

Outbound Destination Sign to Different Runways:
(Black on yellow). In this instance, runways 27 **and** 33 are to your right.

Inbound Destination Sign:
(Black on yellow). In this instance, the military installation is to your right. Other examples are *Cargo, Term* (Terminal), *Ramp*, etc.

AOPA's online course, "*Runway Safety*", is available at AOPA.org.

Mandatory Instruction Signs

These are white on red and denote an entrance to a runway, ILS critical area, or a prohibited

area. This sign indicates that you are on taxiway Alpha and are about to cross (or hold short of) runway 18/36.

No Entry Sign:
(White on red). Aircraft are prohibited. This sign would be found at the entrance to a one-way taxiway, or at the intersection of a road intended for vehicles.

Approach and Hold Sign:
(White on red). Hold here unless instructed by ATC.
At an uncontrolled airport, proceed when a traffic conflict does not exist.

Closed Runway Marking

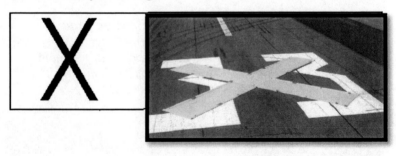

Displaced Thresholds & EMAS

Displacement of a threshold reduces the length of runway available for <u>landings</u>.

The portion of the runway behind a displaced threshold is available for takeoffs - in either direction and for landing rollouts from the opposite direction.

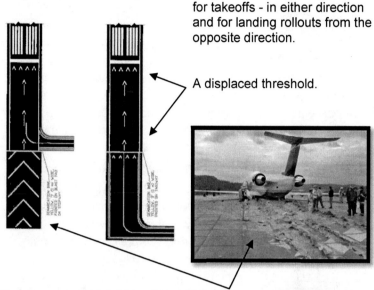

A displaced threshold.

Engineered Materials Arresting System (EMAS)

Areas unusable for taxiing are marked with yellow chevrons. It could be constructed with solid material, or EMAS material. EMAS has the appearance of full strength pavement, but it's actually designed to help *bog down* an aircraft before it runs off the runway.

Airport Lighting

Runway Threshold Lights at the end of the runway are marked with green lights.

Some airports have bi-color lights – <u>green</u> when viewed when you are on approach for landing, and <u>red</u> when viewed while you are rolling out after landing.

Visual Approach Slope Indicator

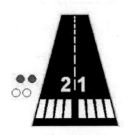

On Glide Path

(VASI) provides safe obstacle clearance within +/- 10 degrees of the extended runway centerline and out to 4 nautical miles from the runway threshold. VASI glide paths are normally set at 3°. To ensure obstacle clearance, some locations are as steep as 4.5°. Three-bar VASI systems provide two visual glide paths, an upper and a lower. The near and middle bar represents a 3° glide path, used by most general aviation pilots. The far and middle are for "high cockpit aircraft", like a B-747.

Precision Approach Path Indicator (PAPI) are visible

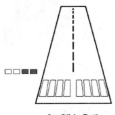

On Glide Path

from about 5 miles during the day and up to 20 miles or more at night. (AIM section 2-1-2). Two white and two red lights indicate that you are on the glide path. Three or more red lights and you're below the glide path. Three or more white lights and you're above the glide path.

Runway End Identifier Lights

(REILs) are pulsating strobe lights on each side of the runway's threshold. These help to distinguish or highlight the runway:
- o   In areas with high levels of non-airport lighting.
- o   In areas with low contrast with the surrounding terrain.
- o   In reduced visibility conditions.

Instrument Approach Runway Lights

When landing on a runway served by an Instrument approach, the runway edge lights change from white to yellow the last 2,000 feet, (or the last half of the runway if it's shorter than 4,000 feet.)

Runway Guard Lights or "Wig-Wag Lights are found
only at runway/taxiway intersections. *They are either:*
- o Elevated flashing lights on both sides of the taxiway, or
- o A row of flashing yellow in-pavement lights.

Clearance Bar Lights are yellow *steady*-burning, in-pavement
lights at taxiway holding positions, making those positions more visible.

Stop Bar Lights are a row of red, *steady*-burning in-pavement
lights installed across the entire taxiway at the runway holding position. Following an ATC clearance to proceed, ATC turns the stop bar lights off and the taxiway centerline lead-on lights are then turned on, guiding you to the takeoff position.

Airport Rotating Beacons *(AIM 2-1-8)*
- o Civilian airport beacon lights flash green and white.
- o A military airport's rotating beacon flashes green followed by two quick flashes of white.
- o A heliport can be identified by its green, yellow, and white beacon.
- o A seaplane base's beacon flashes white and yellow.

Pilot Controlled Lighting (PCL)
While the CTAF is commonly used to activate pilot-controlled lighting, the proper frequency, if different from the CTAF, can be found in the Airport/Facility Directory (A/FD) and on standard instrument approach procedure charts.

Sample A/FD information: "**When twr clsd ACTIVATE HIRL Rwy 10-26 – CTAF**".

Sample Instrument approach procedures chart information:

> **126.1 (CTAF)** Ⓛ

Two Types of PCL

- Single Intensity, non adjustable PCL, where pilots key the microphone three or five times (as specified), within five seconds. Why three or five? Because it's set for one intensity. "3x" indicates that the lighting is set for low intensity, and "5x" means that it's set for medium intensity runway lighting.
- Three level/intensity PCL, where pilots key the microphone within five seconds either:
    - 3 times (for low intensity),
    - 5 times (for medium intensity), or
    - 7 times (for high intensity).

When either type of system is activated, a 15-minute countdown starts, after which the lights turn off unless someone makes the appropriate amount of clicks on the appropriate frequency.

Always initially key the mike 7 times to assure that all controlled lights are turned on to the maximum available intensity. If desired, an intensity adjustment can then be made, (where the capability is provided), or the REIL can be turned off by keying 5 or 3 times. Even when the lights are on, always key the mike as directed when overflying an airport of intended landing, or just prior to entering the final segment of an approach. This will make sure that the aircraft is close enough to activate the system and a full 15 minutes of lighting duration will be available.

 **Flight Guide's** airport information indicates the number of clicks necessary to activate the airfield lighting. "3x" or "5x" for single intensity lighting, or "3x 5x 7x" for three level intensity lighting.

Traffic Patterns – No Tower *(FAR 91.126–127)*
Unless indicated otherwise, all standard turns are to the left. 1,000 feet AGL is the normal pattern altitude, but there may be different altitudes specified for turbines, jets, helicopters, gliders, etc. Check the A/FD. *(AIM 4-3-4)*
Some aircraft don't have a radio, so don't assume that everyone hears you. Standard entry is a 45 to downwind, but some people won't do that. Fly defensively and clear like your life depended on it.

WEATHER

Reports
Forecasts
Wx Briefing Sources
Inflight Wx Resources

Weather Reports

METAR is derived from the French phrase, *"message*

d'observation **mét**éorologique pour l'**a**viation **r**égulière"

METARs are Reported using:
- o VISIBILITY – Statute miles.
- o CLOUD HEIGHTS - AGL.
- o WIND DIRECTION - True.
- o WIND SPEEDS - Knots

METAR Example

METAR KLGA 051853Z 04011KT 1/2SM VCTS SN FZFG BKN003 OVC010 M02/M02 A3006 RMK AO2 TSB40 SLP176 P0002 T10171017=

METAR Decoded

KLGA – weather from LaGuardia, NY

051853Z indicates the day of the month is the **5th** and the time of day is **1853** Zulu time.
04011KT indicates the wind direction and speed – **040 at 11 knots.**
1/2SM indicates the prevailing visibility is ½ statute mile.

VCTS indicates there is a thunderstorm in the **vicinity**, (within 10SM, but beyond 5SM).

SN indicates **snow** is falling at a moderate intensity.
FZFG indicates the presence of **freezing fog**.
BKN003 indicates a **broken** cloud layer at **300 feet AGL**.

OVC010 indicates an **overcast** cloud layer at **1,000 feet AGL.**

M02/M02 indicates the temperature is **minus 2° Celsius** and the dew point is **minus 2°** Celsius.

A3006 indicates the altimeter setting is **30.06**

RMK indicates the **remarks section follows**.

AO2 indicates that the station has an **automated precipitation sensor.**

TSB40 indicates the **thunderstorm began 40 minutes after the top of the hour at 1840 Zulu time.**

SLP176 indicates the current barometric pressure extrapolated to sea level is **1017.6 millibars**

P0002 indicates that **0.02 of precipitation** accumulated during the last hour.

T10171017 indicates the temperature is 29°F, (converted to minus 1.7° Celsius), and the dew point is 29°F, (converted to minus 1.7° Celsius).

= indicates the **end** of the METAR report.

All the METARs in the United States are graphically displayed on the "Weather Depiction Chart"

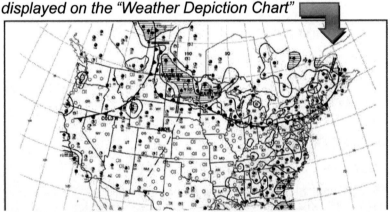

Weather Depiction Chart Symbols

Few clouds (no cloud height is given for "few".

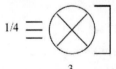

Total obscuration. Vertical vis: 300 feet. ¼ mile fog. The bracket to the right indicates that the report is from an automated system.

Scattered clouds at 2,500 ASL.

 Scattered clouds at 3,000 AGL with 5 miles visibility and haze.

 Broken clouds at 2,000 AGL with 3 miles visibility and continuous rain.

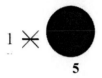 Overcast clouds at 500 AGL with 1 mile visibility and intermittent snow.

 Broken clouds at 1000 AGL with 1 ½ mile visibility and there is also a thunderstorm with rain shower.

 Missing cloud cover or partial obscuration.

IFR areas are depicted by shading inside the contours. Contours without shading depict Marginal VFR (MVFR). Good VFR is reported outside the contours.

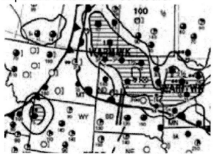

Forecasts

Area Forecasts are issued three times a day and include several areas of the continental US, the Gulf of Mexico, Alaska, Hawaii, and Caribbean. These wide area forecasts help determine the forecast enroute weather, and through interpolation, help determine weather conditions at airports that don't have a TAF.

They report:
- Cloud tops – MSL.
- Times – UTC.
- Winds – Knots.
- Wind Direction –True.
- Distances – Nautical.
- Visibility – Statute.

Area Forecast Example
KANSAS
Western...SCT080 scattered cirrus. Wind southeast G25KT. Outlook: VFR 5:00 MVFR ceiling Mist.
Central...SCT080-100 scattered cirrus. Until 16:00 extreme southern occasional BKN100 top 160. Outlook: VFR 3:00 MVFR ceiling mist.
Eastern...broken-SCT060 top 120 scattered-broken cirrus. Becoming 17:00 to 19:00 SCT040 broken-SCT080 Top 160. Outlook: VFR 2:00 northeastern MVFR ceiling mist.

Terminal Airdrome Forecasts (TAFs) are *valid for an area within a 5 mile radius of the airport.*

TAF Example

KXYZ 241732Z **2418/2524** 11006KT 4SM -SHRA BKN030
FM242300 22006KT 3SM -SHRA OVC030
PROB30 2504/2506 VRB20G35KT 1SM +TSRA BKN015CB

FM 250600 250010KT 4SM -SHRA OVC050
TEMPO 2508/2511 2SM -SHRA OVC030=

TAF Decoded

2418/25: Indicates the valid time of the 30-hour TAF, where 2418 is the 24th day at 1800 UTC, and 2524 is the 25th day at 2400 UTC, (or 0000 UTC on the 26th).

FM242300: Indicates a significant and rapid change to a new set of prevailing conditions, in this case starting at 2300 UTC on the 24th.

PROB30: Indicates the probability of the occurrence of a thunderstorm or other precipitation event. In this case, occurring during the two-hour period between **0400 UTC and 0600 UTC on the 25th.**

TEMPO 2508/2511: Indicates a temporary fluctuation in forecast conditions. In this case, during the two-hour period between 0800 UTC and 0011 UTC on the 25th

"Everybody talks about the weather, but nobody does anything about it."
Mark Twain

Weather Briefing Sources

http://aviationweather.gov/

www.DUATS.com
and
www.DUAT.com

Both **DUATS** and **DUAT** are under contract with the FAA to provide authorized weather briefings.

Winds Aloft are reported in True North. By studying Winds Aloft, you can discover:
- o Temperature inversions.
- o The most favorable cruising altitude.
- o Areas of possible icing, (temps +2° to –20° C).
- o Possible turbulence if there is an abrupt change in wind direction and speed at different altitudes.

```
000
FDUW01 KWBC 110159
DATA BASED ON 110000Z
VALID 110600Z   FOR USE 0500-0900Z. TEMPS NEG ABV 24000


FT  3000   6000    9000   12000   18000   24000  30000   34
PHX 2712 2916+08 3015-01 2913-08 3030-21 3236-34 304642 285
PRC         3113-01 3016-08 3225-21 3443-34 335144 313
TUS      3115+07 2714-01 2617-06 2839-18 2759-31 257638 268
ALS                 1714+00 1758-16 1960-30 198843 207
DEN         0214+01 0708-04 1532-15 1744-27 205743 206
GJT         0509+01 0505-07 1722-20 1755-32 166848 184
PUB         9900+11 1817+02 1841-16 2056-29 207142 205
BOI      3605+10 9900+02 9900-06 3611-19 3522-30 353446 343
```

- o Over DEN at 12,000 feet, the wind is from 070° at 8 knots; temp -4°C.
- o Winds are not forecast for levels less than 1,500 feet above a station. For instance the high stations such as PRC, DEN, GJT and PUB don't forecast winds until 9,000 feet, and ALS starts forecasting at 12,000 feet.
- o Over GJT at 18,000 feet, the wind is from 170° at 22 knots; -20° C.
- o Over BOI at 9,000 feet, **"9900"** = Wind is light and variable.
- o **7510-41** – The **seven** indicates winds over 100 knots. (One subtracts 5 from first number and inserts a 1 in front of the 3rd number) = Wind from 250° @ 110knots; temp is -41° C
- o At and above 30,000 feet, the minus sign is not used. One is to assume a negative temperature.

Convective Outlook

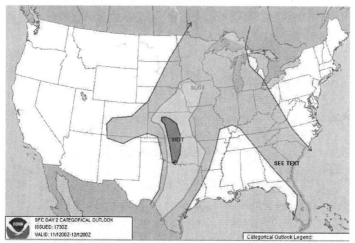

A Convective Outlook is issued five times daily, and forecasts the chances of thunderstorms as either:

- o General (shaded areas which are not labeled),
- o Slight (Labeled SLGT),
- o Moderate (Labeled MDT)
- o High.

SIGMETs *(SIGnificant Meteorological Information)*

Convective SIGMETs (Thunderstorms) are issued every hour at 55 minutes past the hour, in the continental US. If no convective SIGMET is forecast, then the region issues "CONVECTIVE SIGMET NONE". They are valid a maximum of two hours. *Convective SIGMETs include:*

- o Lines of thunderstorms or areas of thunderstorms covering 40% or more of a 3,000 square mile or larger area.
- o Embedded thunderstorms (obscured), and severe thunderstorms, if they are expected to endure more than 30 minutes.

Severe thunderstorms include tornadoes, thunderstorms, hail, and wind gusts greater or equal to 50 knots.

SIGMETs warn of significant weather, other than convective activity, that is hazardous to all aircraft. SIGMETs may be issued at any time, and have a maximum forecast period of 4 hours.

SIGMETs are issued for:
- Severe icing.
- Severe turbulence.
- Clear air turbulence.
- Sand and dust storms.
- Volcanic ash (valid up to six hours).
- Large areas of IFR conditions and possible mountain obscuration, or sustained surface winds greater or equal to 30 knots.
- In Alaska and Hawaii, SIGMETs are also issued for tornadoes, a line of thunderstorms, embedded thunderstorms, or hail greater than or equal to 3/4 inch.

AIRMETs - *(AIRman's METeorological Information)*

These advise of weather that is potentially hazardous to all aircraft, but not meeting SIGMET criteria.

AIRMETs are *widespread, affecting* an area of at least 3,000 square miles at any one time. That's the combined size of Rhode Island and Delaware.

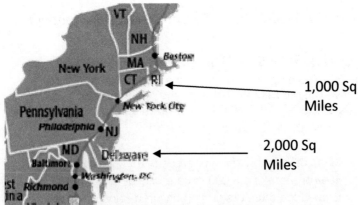

An AIRMET is a "time smeared forecast" valid for a six hour period. If the total area to be affected during the forecast period is very large, it could be that only a small portion of the total area would be affected at any one time.

AIRMETs are issued for:

- **Instrument Flight Rules (IFR) or Mountain Obscuration -**
  - That means that ceilings less than 1000 feet and/or visibility less than 3 miles is affecting over 50% of the area at one time.
  - Extensive mountain obscuration.
- **Turbulence**
  - Moderate Turbulence.
  - Sustained surface winds of greater than 30 knots at the surface.
- **Icing**
  - Moderate icing.
  - Freezing levels.

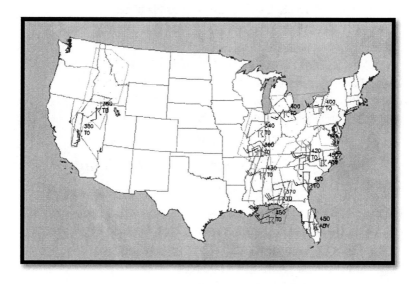

Inflight Weather Resources

Automated Weather Observing Systems (AWOS) & Automated Weather Surface Observing Systems (ASOS) facts:

- o If broadcast on a VOR frequency, it is designated by an "A" in the NAVAID's frequency box.
- o Otherwise, its frequency is listed on the chart by the airport's data.
  - **AWOS-A:** Simply reports the altimeter setting.
  - **AWOS-1:** Reports altimeter setting, wind data, temperature/dew point, and density altitude, (when it exceeds field elevation by more than 1,000 feet).
  - **AWOS-2:** Like AWOS-1, plus visibility.
  - **AWOS-3:** Like AWOS-2, plus cloud/ceiling data, (below 12,000 feet AGL).
  - **ASOS:** Like AWOS-3, plus precipitation.

When checking in with an approach controller for landing at an airport with ASOS or AWOS, simply include that you have the landing airport's "one minute weather".

En-route Flight Advisory Service (EFAS), or "Flight Watch" – EFAS can provide weather

updates, PIREPs, and advisories. Call them on 122.0 (below 18,000 feet MSL). Use the ATC facility's name, "Los Angeles Flight Watch", not the Flight Service name. *EFAS is available:*

- o Above 5,000 AGL to 17,500 MSL.
- o 7 days a week, 6 am to 10 pm local.

In many areas, it's possible to make contact well below 5,000' AGL. Give it a try before you start a climb.

Providing a PIREP to EFAS, 122.0

The Required Stuff, PIREP:

- o **LOCATION** (Nearest VOR or Airport).
- o **TIME**—ZULU or minutes ago.
- o **ALTITUDE** (MSL).
- o **A/C TYPE.**

Optional Stuff, PIREP:

- **CLOUD COVERAGE** - (CLR, FEW, SCT, BKN, OVC), **TYPE** - (Cirrus, Cumulus, Stratus), & **HEIGHT** - (Bases & Tops should be expressed in feet MSL).
- **VISIBILITY** - (in statute miles), & **RESTRICTIONS** - (Haze, Mist, Fog, Dust, Sand, Smoke, Spray, Volcanic Ash).
- **PRECIP TYPE** - (Rain, drizzle, snow, and hail), & **INTENSITY** - (Light, moderate, or heavy).
- **TEMP** - (Celsius).
- **WIND** - (Direction & Speed in knots)
- **TURBULENCE** - (Light, light chop, moderate, moderate chop, severe, or extreme).
- **ICING** - (Trace, light, moderate, or severe).
- **REMARKS.**

AOPA's online PIREP course, "*Sky Spotter*" and several of their Aviation Weather courses – "*Weather Wise*", are available at AOPA.org.

Transcribed Weather En route Broadcast (TWEB)

TWEBs are becoming rare, but if you find one:

- They are recorded on tape, and broadcast on selected VOR frequencies.
- They are designated by a "T" in the NAVAID's frequency box.
- They are issued 3 times each day, providing sky cover, visibility, winds, & NOTAMS.
- Up to five reporting station's weather observations can be included in a TWEB.

Hazardous In-flight Weather Advisory Service (HIWAS)

- o Available on select VOR frequencies.
- o Designated by a circled "H" in the NAVAID's frequency box.

In areas serviced by HIWAS, centers (ARTCC), tower facilities and flight service stations will not broadcast in-flight weather advisories. They will, however, broadcast that an advisory has been published, and tell you to tune in to HIWAS for details.

Calling Flight Service (Radio)

By Debby Colvin, Lockheed Martin Quality Assurance Specialist.

To ensure a quick radio response from flight service, here are some suggestions:

- o On initial call, always give the frequency and your current location using NAVAIDs or airport references with your request.
- o Always use your full aircraft identification on initial call-up.
- o If you are unsure of the name of your nearest flight service station, provide the geographical area of your position. Rather than broadcasting for "Any Radio, N12345," you should transmit, "Radio near Greenwood, Mississippi, N12345."

The average pilot, despite the somewhat swaggering exterior, is very much capable of such feelings as love, affection, intimacy, and caring.

Those feelings just don't involve anyone else.

66

FLIGHT PLANNING

Flight Service
Internet Planning Tools
Clouds
Weather Codes
Ice
Aircraft Loading
Density Altitude &
Tailwinds (Takeoff)
Flight Plan Format

Flight Service Resources

> *To speak to a briefer, call:*
> **1-800-WX-BRIEF**
> **(1-800-992-7433)**

The briefer will need to know the following:

1) VFR or IFR.
2) Registration Number.
3) Aircraft Type.
4) Departure airport's ID.
5) Departure time (ZULU).
6) Altitude.
7) Route.
8) Destination airport's ID.
9) Time en route.

IFR CLEARANCE DELIVERY

(888) 766-8267
888-SPOT-BOT

To report a problem with Flight Service, call:
1-888-FLT-SRVC

Ask the briefer, "Are there any Temporary Flight Restrictions (TFRs)?" (This puts it on tape).

Flight Service Briefing Types
An Outlook Briefing is a synopsis. Its forecast range is more than 6 hours out and up to 5 days ahead.

Standard (6 Hours or Less from Takeoff)
- Current and forecast weather.
- Adverse conditions.
- Winds aloft.
- NOTAMS & TFRs.
- "VFR not recommended".

Abbreviated
This updates a previously received Standard briefing.

You must ask for specific:
- Weather forecasts.
- NOTAMS.
- TFRs.

TIBS (Telephone Information Briefing Service)
Call Flt Svc (800-WX-BRIEF), then press "3" or say "TIBS." Also, TIBS line: 877-4TIBS-WX. Includes SIGMETs, AIRMETs METARs, TAFs, winds aloft. (This recording does not constitute a weather briefing).

Lockheed Martin Tips, Reference www.afss.com
"Early morning hours, 06:00-10:00, are our busiest times. If your schedule permits, call before or after this time.
File your flight plan with flight service during off hours, well in advance of your scheduled departure. (If you plan to depart at 07:00 local time, file your flight plan the night before)."

AOPA's online course, "*A Pilot's Guide to Flight Service*", is available at AOPA.org.

FAA Authorized Internet Briefing Sites

The FAA has authorized two replacements for the telephone weather briefing:

www.DUAT.COM. Full weather brief and NOTAMS – files your flight plans - FREE

Also see ***DUAT.com/mobile***

 DTC Duat's SmartPhone app

www.*DUATS*.com
Full weather brief and NOTAMS - files flight plans — FREE.

Internet Flight Planning Tools

Also see
Aeroplanner.com/MOBILE
(Mobile requires a Premium membership).
Flight Planning, File flight plans - IFR & VFR (uses DUATS), Weather, NOTAMS, Airport Directory/Lodging, Approach Charts, and Logbook.

AOPA.org (AOPA membership required)
Flight Planning, file flight plans, weather, NOTAMS, Airport Directory, Approach Charts. ***AOPA Airports SmartPhone app***.

 Also see *FltPlan.com/PDA* — FREE Flight Planning, file IFR flight plans, check previous clearances for the same route, checks RAIM (IFR flights). After you file, you can read your actual ATC clearance.

 Weather, NOTAMS, Airport Directory, Approach Charts. Flight tracking, tell the FBO that you're coming, and more. *FltPlan Mobile* and **FltPlan.com FltDeck Airport/FBO Guide** SmartPhone/iPad apps.

FltPlan.com is an FAA approved and certified source of Weather and Notams. It is a QICP (Qualified Internet Communications Provider) weather service.

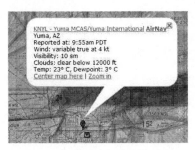 *RunwayFinder.com* FREE. METAR, TAF VFR, MVFR, IFR, LIFR TFRs

AirNav.com FREE. Fuel Prices / Planning trips with cheapest or quickest fuel stops Airport Information + NAVAIDs & fixes. Lodging, and AIRBOSS fuel program.

 AirNav FBO iPhone app – small annual fee, but FREE to AirBoss® members.

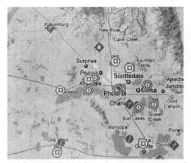

Maps.AvnWx.com

FREE. TFRs, SIGMETS, AIRMETS, winds, route briefing, NEXRAD radar, METAR/TAF/PIREPS, temps aloft, NOTAMS, airport details, & A/FD.

Adds.AviationWeather.gov
FREE
Every weather tool you can imagine, including those using powerful JAVA programs.

The GA Pilot's Pre-Flight Web Site
NavMonster.com

Also see
NavMonster.com/mobile
Weather, winds aloft, charts, airport information, and fuel prices, etc.

Flightguide.com

An online version of the FLIGHT GUIDE – Great resource for planning a flight, and getting the latest information for updating your *FLIGHT GUIDE*. Includes airport diagrams, pattern altitudes, frequencies, FBOs, restaurants and lodging.

ForeFlight *iPhone and iPad* app – *does everything. Includes GPS flight following on charts.*

Clouds and What to Expect

Nimbostratus: Diffused, generally grey, shapeless, and very low, (less than 1,500 feet AGL). Think of a dreary day. Expect poor visibility, unstable air and light mist or drizzle.

Mammatus: Good visibility, wind shear; showers and thunderstorms.

Lenticular: When near a mountain, expect up and down drafts, (mountain waves).

Cumulonimbus: Unstable air and good visibility. Associated with a thunderstorm, so expect a rough ride.

Cirrus: Thin, wispy clouds composed of ice and blown by high winds into long streamers. Cirrus clouds are usually white and indicate fair to pleasant weather. Expect Stable air.

Virga: This is precipitation that evaporates before reaching the ground. Expect unstable air and microbursts; down and up drafts.

Weather Codes		
BC Patches	FZ Freezing	SA Sand
BL Blowing	GR Hail	SG Snow Grains
BR Mist	GS Hail/Snow Pellets	SH Showers
CB Cumulonimbus	HZ Haze	SN Snow
DR Low Drifting	IC Ice Crystals	+SN Heavy Snow
DS Dust Storm	MI Shallow	SQ Squall
DU Dust	PE Ice Pellets	SS Sand Storm
DZ Drizzle	PO Dust/Sand Whirls	TC Towering CB
+FX Tornado	PR Partial	TS Thunderstorms
FC Funnel Cloud	PY Spray	UP Unknown Precip.
FG Fog	RA Rain	VA Volcanic Ash
FU Smoke	-RA Light Rain	

Estimating the Freezing Level

The average lapse rate per thousand feet is 2°C.
If XYZ airport has a field elevation of 1,000 feet MSL, and the current temperature at XYZ is 10°C, then the freezing level can be found at 6,000 feet MSL.

6,000 feet MSL	0°C
5,000 feet MSL	2°C
4,000 feet MSL	4°C
3,000 feet MSL	6°C
2,000 feet MSL	8°C
XYZ Airport, 1,000 feet MSL	10°C

Induction Icing

Flying in snow can create it, blocking air filters, static ports, and the air ducts that provide engine cooling.
Less engine air flow suffocates the engine and the fuel/air mixture becomes richer.

Go to *http://aircrafticing.grc.nasa.gov*
or perform an internet search for "*NASA aircraft icing training*".

Carburetor Ice is most likely to form when the temps are -5°C to 15°C, and as warm as 30°C if the air is humid. The temperature of the air passing through the carburetor can drop as much as 60° in a nanosecond, squeezing water vapor out of the air. When the temperature in the carburetor reaches 0° C or below, frost or ice forms.

How do you know if you have Carburetor ice?
- A **fixed pitch** propeller's <u>RPM</u> drops.
- A **constant speed** propeller's <u>manifold pressure</u> drops.

USE CARB HEAT when you have a rough running engine.
DON'T USE CARB HEAT when taking off or climbing. It causes detonation.

All the Frost, Snow & Ice Must Go

Don't expect loose snow to blow off. Rough frost on a wing spoils the flow of air, causing the airflow to slow. This causes early airflow separation and a loss of lift. The smallest amount of frost can prevent an aircraft from becoming airborne. Even if you manage to take off, your aircraft could stall in the climb.

Reducing the Risk of Airframe Icing

Avoid FZRA (freezing rain) and FZDZ (freezing drizzle). Convective SIGMETs imply severe icing potential. A 50% relative humidity may imply a high probability of icing.

As you get closer to the center of a low pressure system, moisture moves upwards faster, resulting in icing conditions at higher altitudes.

Lack of Ice Protection

If you don't have an ice removal / prevention system, then you must seek warmer air. How warm? At 3°C, the ice will slowly dissipate. An OAT of 4°C or more will rapidly melt the ice!

Encountering Freezing Rain?

Since freezing rain requires a temperature inversion, you might find warmer air if you initiate a climb.

Aircraft Loading

Aft Center of Gravity (CG) Characteristics

- o Less wing loading = a slower stall speed.
- o Reduced drag. A smaller angle of attack is required to maintain level flight, so the cruise speed is higher.
- o Less stable & less controllable.

IF THE CG IS aft of the AIRCRAFT'S AFT CG limit:
The aircraft could stall after takeoff or Go-Around. (Not enough elevator authority to recover).

RULES AND LAWS
Rules are made by those who are trying to keep you safe. Laws of Physics are set by the Almighty. You may find it necessary to suspend a Rule, but you can never suspend a Law.

Forward Center of Gravity (CG) Characteristics

- o Increased wing loading = a higher stall speed.
- o Increased drag and a greater angle of attack to maintain level flight, so the cruise speed is slower.
- o More stable & controllable.

IF THE CG IS forward of the AIRCRAFT'S FORWARD CG limit:
- o It's harder to rotate, and flare.
- o Takeoff rolls are longer.

Calculating
Weight & Moment

FORMULA: (Weight) X (Moment Arm) = Moment			
	Weight	Arm	Moment
Airplane's Basic Empty Weight			
Pilot			
Front Seat Passenger			
Rear seat Passenger(s)			
Fuel_____gal			
Cargo			
Total Weight		Total Moment	

WEIGHTS	
AvGas	**6 lb / gal**
Jet A	**6.75 lb / gal**
Oil	**1.9 lb / qt**
Water	**8.3 lb / gal**

Takeoff and Landing Distances

DENSITY ALTITUDE CHART

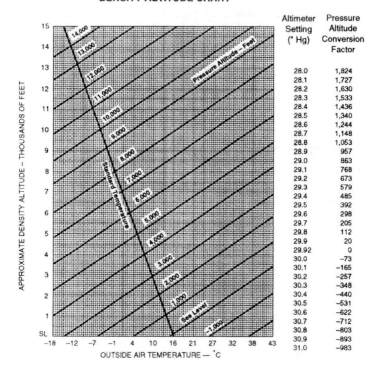

Altimeter Setting (" Hg)	Pressure Altitude Conversion Factor
28.0	1,824
28.1	1,727
28.2	1,630
28.3	1,533
28.4	1,436
28.5	1,340
28.6	1,244
28.7	1,148
28.8	1,053
28.9	957
29.0	863
29.1	768
29.2	673
29.3	579
29.4	485
29.5	392
29.6	298
29.7	205
29.8	112
29.9	20
29.92	0
30.0	–73
30.1	–165
30.2	–257
30.3	–348
30.4	–440
30.5	–531
30.6	–622
30.7	–712
30.8	–803
30.9	–893
31.0	–983

A RULE YOU CAN LIVE WITH

AOPA Air Safety Institute recommends that you use the 50/50 rule for takeoff correction. That is:

Correcting for altitude and temperature, determine the takeoff distance that's required to clear a 50 foot obstacle. Then, increase that number by an additional 50%.

Higher Density Altitude

There is less thrust:

- Slower takeoff acceleration.
- Longer takeoff rolls.
- Decreased climb rate.

Higher density altitude increases the landing Ground Speed. You'll land at the same indicated airspeed, but because the true airspeed is greater, you'll have a longer landing distance.

Taking Off With a Tailwind

For every 10% of the takeoff speed, a tailwind will increase the ground run by about 21%. **FOR EXAMPLE:** Let's assume that you plan to lift off at 60 knots, and the zero-wind charted takeoff ground roll is 1,300 feet. A 6 knot tailwind, (10% of the 60 knot takeoff speed), will increase your charted 1,300 ground roll by 21%, or 273 feet.

Fickle Headwinds

Winds have a mind of their own, and can change quickly with altitude, or simply disappear. Never count on a headwind to ensure your takeoff!

Crosswinds

The required control surface deflection and tire scrubbing add extra drag, and increase the ground roll.

Exceeding Maximum Takeoff Weight (MTOW)

Excess weight and its consequences:

- Reduced structural load safety factor.
- Reduced acceleration, higher takeoff speed, and longer takeoff distance.
- Reduced rate and angle of climb.
- Reduced cruising speed and range.
- Lower stalling speed and reduced maneuverability.
- Higher landing speed and extended landing distance.
- The aircraft may not leave the ground when you attempt a take-off.

Flight Plan Format

1. Type (VFR, IFR, DVFR)	2. Aircraft ID	3. Aircraft type / Special Equipment	4. TAS
5. Dept Point	6. Dept Time Proposed (Z) Actual (Z)	7. Cruising Alt	
8. Route of Flight			
9. Destination Airport & City	10. ETE	11. Remarks	
12. Fuel On Board (Hours & Minutes)	13. Alternate Airport(s)	14. Pilots Name, Address & Telephone and Home Base	
15. Number on Board		16. Aircraft Color	
17. Destination Contact/Telephone (Optional)			

To Convert From	To ZULU Time
EST	+5
EDT	+4
CST	+6
CDT	+5
MST	+7
MDT	+6
PST	+8
PDT	+7

See the next page for a list of the *"Most Common General Aviation Special Equipment Suffixes"*.

Most Common General Aviation Special Equipment Suffixes	
/X	No Transponder
/T	Transponder, but no Altitude Encoding (Mode C)
/U	Transponder with Mode C
/D	DME, no Transponder
/B	DME& Transponder but no Altitude Encoding (Mode C)
/A	DME & Transponder with Mode C
/I	RNAV or LORAN or INS & Transponder with Mode C
/G	GPS – Enroute & Approach, & Transponder with Mode C

The ultimate responsibility of the pilot is to fulfill the dreams of the countless millions of earthbound ancestors who could only stare skyward and wish.

AOPA's online courses, *"Accident Case Study: Cross Country Crisis"* and *"Accident Case Study: VFR into IMC"*, are available at AOPA.org

THE FLIGHT REVIEW

Are you Familiar with Your Aircraft?

Engine out glide speed for maximum range _____.

Make and horsepower of your engine _____.

Fuel capacity _____.

Usable gallons of fuel _____.

Minimum & maximum oil capacity _____.

Your oil type and weight _____.

Max oil temp and pressure_____.

Max demonstrated crosswind (limit) _____.

How many people will it carry with a full load of fuel? _____.

Baggage compartment limit _____.

Sea Level takeoff distance _____.

Vso _____ Stall speed in the landing configuration.

Vs _____ Clean stall speed.

Vy _____ Best rate of climb speed.

Normal climb-out speed _____.

Vx _____ Best angle of climb speed.

Normal approach-to land speed _____.

Vle _____ Max landing gear extended speed, or the speed it can be flown with the gear down.

Vlo _____ Max landing gear operating speed.

Do you know the backup system for lowering the gear?

Vfe _____ Max flap extension speed.

Va _____ Maneuvering speed.

Vno _____ Maximum structural cruising speed in turbulence (end of the green arc and beginning of the yellow arc). Yellow arc speeds are for smooth air only.

Vne _____ Never exceed speed (RED LIINE).

Soft Field Takeoff

Use recommended Takeoff Flaps. With the yoke as far aft as you can hold it, taxi onto the runway without stopping. Once lined up on the centerline, apply full power with the yoke still in the full aft position.
As you add power, you'll also need to add right rudder. As the nose wheel comes off the ground, you might need to reduce backpressure a bit to avoid scraping the tail.

The idea is to get unstuck from the runway at the first possible opportunity and then build up airspeed in ground effect before attempting to climb out. The main wheels will lift off at a lower airspeed than normal. As soon as all three wheels are off the ground, relax the yoke a bit to increase climb speed.

Because of the high power setting and high angle of attack, as soon as you're airborne, you'll need additional right rudder to keep the nose tracking straight. Don't try to climb out of ground effect until you're at best rate of climb speed, (Vy).

Soft Field Landing

The objective is to land as gently as possible on the main gear and to keep the nose wheel off the ground as long as possible during the rollout to minimize the chances of becoming stuck, or flipping over, if the nose wheel digs in.

Fly a stabilized approach with full flaps. Just before touchdown, add a little power, (just slightly above idle), to reduce the sink rate and to provide more <u>elevator</u> authority, while keeping the nose wheel off the runway.

After your gentle, nose-high touchdown, maintain enough backpressure to hold the nose wheel off the runway as long as possible without scraping the tail. You won't have nose wheel steering with the nose wheel off the surface, so you'll need rudder input to maintain directional control.

Eventually, the nose wheel should touchdown smoothly while holding the yoke full aft, minimizing the weight on the nose wheel.

Exit the runway with the <u>yoke</u> held full aft and, local conditions permitting, taxi without stopping to your tie down spot.

Short Field Takeoff

Used when you need to get off the ground in the minimum distance and climb steeply to clear obstacles. Set flaps for takeoff. When you taxi onto the runway, DON'T WASTE RUNWAY.

Hold the brakes and apply full power. Check the engine instruments and tachometer, to ensure that you have full power!

Release the brakes and rotate normally, commencing a climb out at the recommended obstacle clearance speed or best angle of climb speed, (Vx). This is a higher angle of attack than the one you see during a normally climb.

You'll need additional right rudder to keep the nose tracking straight.

Pay attention to your airspeed indicator.

After clearing the obstacle, lower the nose slightly and accelerate to best rate of climb speed, (<u>Vy</u>). Now you can retract the gear and the flaps.

Short Field Landing

The objective is to clear obstacles on final, land, and stop in the minimum distance possible.

Stabilize the aircraft with full-flaps at the recommended short field approach speed for your airplane. That's usually 1.3 x Vso (stall speed configured). This is usually a few knots slower than normal approach speed.

Once obstacles have been cleared and landing is assured, reduce power to idle and continue to descend at the minimum recommended speed until you're ready to flare.

After touchdown, retract the flaps while applying maximum braking. Raising the flaps transfers the load from the wings to the wheels, and allows you to brake harder. Take care that you do not lock the wheels and skid.

Bring the airplane to a full stop before exiting the runway.

It can be a firm landing, as long as the main gear touches down first and there's no bounce.

Avoiding Wake Turbulence (AIM 7-3-6)

- o All aircraft generate some wake turbulence through their wing-tip vortices. The greatest vortex is generated by a heavy, clean, and slow aircraft.
- o If landing behind a large aircraft on the same runway, stay at or above its flight path. Note its touchdown point and land BEYOND that point.
- o If landing behind a departing large aircraft, note its rotation point and land well BEFORE that point.
- o If departing behind a large aircraft on the same runway, note its rotation point and rotate BEFORE that point. Climb ABOVE and UPWIND of its flight path.

"Airplanes are never impressed by the flying credentials in your wallet."
James Price

When Things Go Wrong

Ammeter, Positive Indication

AFTER STARTING - POSSIBLE CAUSES:

- Battery may be recharging after starting (That's normal).
- If you see a full scale charge for more than one minute, then the starter is probably still engaged. (That's not normal).

SOLUTION: Shut down the engine.

DURING FLIGHT - PROBIBLE CAUSE:

- Faulty voltage regulator, allowing the alternator to overcharge the battery.

SOLUTION: Reset the system by turning the Master Switch OFF, and then ON.

If the problem continues, the battery could explode and you could damage your electrical system.

- Pull the Alternator Field CB.
- Turn all non-essential equipment OFF.
- Get the aircraft on the ground as soon as possible because the battery is now the only source of electrical power.

Ammeter, Negative Indication

AFTER STARTING OR IN FLIGHT – POSSIBLE CAUSES:

- The alternator isn't working.
- The system is overloaded.
- The battery is not charging.

SOLUTION:

Check Master Switch ON and Alternator Circuit Breaker IN.

If THE Master Switch is ON and the Alternator CB is IN, and still there's a problem:

- Turn the alternator OFF and pull the Alternator Field CB.
- All non-essential equipment OFF.
- Get the aircraft on the ground as soon as possible because the battery is now the only source of electrical power.

Oil Temp Normal, Oil Pressure Low

POSSIBLE CAUSES:
- Insufficient oil.
- If oil temps remain normal, it could be a clogged oil pressure relief valve or malfunctioning oil pressure gauge.

SOLUTION: Land as soon as possible and have it checked.

Engine Fire on the Ground

Continue to crank the engine. (Flames and excess fuel will be sucked into the carburetor).

IF THE ENGINE STARTS:
Add power for a few seconds, and then, shut it down.

IF THE ENGINE DOES NOT START:
- Throttle – Full OPEN.
- Mixture – CUTOFF.
- Continue to crank the engine.

IF THE FIRE CONTINUES:
- Ignition – OFF.
- Master Switch – OFF.
- Fuel Selector – OFF.

> Priorities when things go wrong:
> - Aviate
> - Navigate
> - Communicate

Engine Fire in Flight

- Mixture – CUTOFF.
- Fuel selector – OFF.
- Master Switch – OFF.
- Cabin heat & air vents – OFF & CLOSED.
- Execute a forced landing.

Partial Loss of Power

1) Attain and maintain glide airspeed.
2) Select an emergency landing area or airfield, and remain over it.
3) *CHECK:*
   - Carburetor Heat.
   - Fuel – If necessary, switch tanks.
   - Mixture.
   - Primer, (if installed) – Ensure that it's all the way in and locked.
   - Magnetos – check in all three positions.

Forced Landing, Engine Failure

Do you know the glide ratio for your airplane? If you're 3,000 feet AGL, how far can you glide?

Establish best glide speed, then Check:
- o Fuel selector
- o Mixture RICH
- o Carb Heat – ON
- o Magnetos

If the engine fails to start, select a landing site and:
- o Variable pitch props – full decrease
- o Transmit on 121.5 or current controller
- o Squawk 7700
- o Seat belts – Secure
- o Fuel – OFF
- o Mixture – Cutoff
- o Flaps and gear as needed. If it's a soft field, you may want to consider landing gear up
- o Door – Ajar

The Impossible Turn

If your engine fails after takeoff, consider this: Unless you are at 1,000 feet AGL, or you have already started a turn, it's safer to forget about trying *"The Impossible Turn"* and landing at the airport. What you see outside your windscreen is a safer place to land.

Reference the AOPA Air Safety Institute Nall Report: Most maneuvering related crashes are fatal. But only about 10% of forced landing accidents involve a fatality. You're better off maintaining control of the aircraft all the way to the ground, even if you're landing off airport. This greatly increases the chances of surviving.

Glide Distance is defined as half the distance from your airplane, to the nearest emergency landing field.

Carb Ice is most likely to form when the temps are -5°C to 15°C; 30°C if the air is humid. The temperature of the air passing through the carburetor can drop as much as 60° in a nanosecond! Water vapor is squeezed out by this cooling, and if the temperature in the carburetor reaches 0° C or below, the moisture becomes frost or ice in the carburetor.

How do you know if you have Carburetor Ice?
- **Fixed pitch propeller** – <u>RPM</u> drops.
- **Constant speed propeller** – <u>Manifold</u> pressure drops.

When to Notify the NTSB (NTSB 830)
You should notify the NTSB if:
- You've had an aircraft accident.
- You've had a flight control system malfunction.
- A crewmember is unable to perform normal duties.
- A turbine engine has a failure of its structural components.
- You've had an in-flight fire.
- You've experienced an aircraft collision in flight.
- You've had property damage, (other than the aircraft), estimated to exceed $25,000.
- There is an overdue aircraft and you believe that it has been in an accident.

Should You Notify NTSB?
This *iPhone app may help you make your decision.*

Lost Communications, Landing VFR at a Controlled Airport

- o Remain outside or above Class D airspace until you determine the direction of traffic and runway in use.
- o Squawk 7600 before entering Class D airspace.
- o Enter the traffic pattern downwind on "a 45", and fly a typical pattern for landing.
- o Look for Tower's light gun signals.

ATC Light Signals (FAR 91.125)

COLOR & SIGNAL TYPE	ON THE GROUND	IN FLIGHT
STEADY GREEN	Cleared for T.O.	Cleared to land
FLASHING GREEN	Cleared to taxi	Return for landing (to be followed by a STEADY GREEN LIGHT)
STEADY RED	Stop	Give way to other aircraft and continue circling
FLASHING RED	Taxi clear of runway in use	Airport is UNSAFE – Do not land
FLASHING WHITE	Return to starting point	N/A
ALTERNATING RED & GREEN	GENERAL WARNING – USE EXTREME CAUTION	

To acknowledge a light signal:
Day, in flight – Rock wings. Day, on ground – Move aileron or rudder.
Night – Flash landing light or nav lights.

Lost Communications, Landing VFR at an Uncontrolled Airport

- o Overfly the airport 500 feet above pattern altitude.
- o Look for traffic, wind direction, and runway in use.
- o Enter the traffic pattern downwind on "a 45", and fly a typical pattern for landing.

"Mistakes are inevitable in aviation, especially when one is still learning new things. The trick is to not make the mistake that will kill you."
Stephen Coonts, Author

"Aviation in itself is not inherently dangerous. But to an even greater degree than the sea, it is terribly unforgiving of any carelessness, incapacity or neglect."

Capt. A. G. Lamplugh, (1895-1955)

LOST
and
FOUND

To Avoid Becoming Lost:

- Use your GPS.
- Have spare batteries near you, and <u>not</u> in the baggage area.
- Keep a chart open, and continually update your position.
- Use the VOR receivers <u>and</u> the GPS. Not one or the other.
- Note the time that you're over checkpoints.
- Note the difference between forecast and actual winds.
- Practice pilotage, using your eyes to check for landmarks.

Lost? Don't Panic and Check Your Fuel. If you have lots of it, reorient yourself and regain situational awareness.

If You're Hopelessly Lost:

- Gain altitude if possible so you can get a better look at the ground. You'll also have better VOR reception.
- Note your compass heading. Write it down, and note the time.
- Locate your last known position on the chart.
- What heading were you flying that took you there? Was the landmark on, or off your course? How long ago did you pass the landmark?
- Draw a line from your last known position on the heading you're on — out to where you should be now. If you're flying 120 knots, (that's 2 nm per minute). If you've been flying 10 minutes, you're 20 nm past the last known position.
- Draw a 45° arc each side of the new position, and try to figure out where you are.

You Can Also:
Tune in two VORs, and cross the radials to determine your location. If you only find one VOR, don't panic. Fly to it, and then you'll know your exact location.

Re-printed with permission from *Trade-A-Plane*, 2nd August Issue, 2002

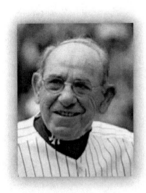

"If you don't know where you are going, chances are you will end up someplace else."
Yogi Berra

If Lost and Fuel is Low:

Taking QUICK action is very important. If there's any doubt, declare an emergency and get help.
Call a known ATC frequency or 121.5, (the emergency frequency). Flight Service, civilian and military control towers, approach controls and centers – all monitor 121.5.

Set your power to best economy and maximum endurance.

Surrounding terrain, obstacles ahead and the amount of daylight remaining, all play a role in determining the best response.
Get it on the ground. Any port in a storm!

The 4 C's

Climb. *You'll have* better signal reception.

Communicate. Call for help. You don't need to declare an emergency. Call on 121.5, or you can contact a tower in the vicinity, and ask for the frequency of the controlling ATC facility, (center, approach, or departure control). You can also call flight service on 122.2.

Confess. Ask for a position confirmation.

Comply with ATC's directions.

Now that you're found, make sure you have enough fuel to continue to your destination. If not, land and refuel.

"You've never been lost until you've been lost at Mach 3."

Paul F. Crickmore, Author, *"SR-71 Blackbird - Lockheed's Mach 3 Hot Shot"*

Minimum Fuel vs. Emergency Fuel

Minimum fuel: You cannot accept any delays
Emergency fuel: You need priority handling

"Mix ignorance with arrogance at low altitude and the results are almost guaranteed to be spectacular."
Bruce Landsberg,
AOPA Air Safety Institute

CORRECTING MAG COMPASS ERRORS

Mag Compass Turning Errors

Undershoot **N**orth, and Overshoot **SOUTH**

- o **UN** - When turning to the NORTH, the magnetic compass UNDERSHOOTS. You should rollout BEFORE the desired heading. If you're turning from a NORTHERLY heading, the compass LAGs, and actually starts a turn in the opposite direction.

- o **OS** - When turning to the SOUTH, the compass OVERSHOOTS. You should rollout PAST the desired heading. If you're turning from a SOUTHERLY heading, the compass LEADs, and starts a turn more rapidly in the correct direction.

When turning to an EAST or WEST heading, there's no lagging or leading. You should roll out on the desired heading.

Acceleration and Deceleration Errors

Accelerate **N**orth & **D**ecelerate **S**outh

- o **AN** - If you're flying EASTERLY or WESTERLY, and airspeed is **ACCELERATING,** the compass will indicate a turn to the **NORTH**.

- o **DS** - If you're flying EASTERLY or WESTERLY, and airspeed is **DECELERATING,** the compass will indicate a turn to the **SOUTH**.

MAG DIP

This causes compass errors when you turn, accelerate, and decelerate. The rollout correction for Northerly and Southerly turns is approximately equal to your latitude.
 If you are flying in the southern half of the United States, use 30° as a rollout correction. If flying in the northern half, use 40°. Refine it when you roll out of your turn.

Aviation Safety Reporting System (ASRS)

http://asrs.arc.nasa.gov

ASRS collects aviation safety incident and situation reports from pilots and controllers. These reports are submitted voluntarily and with anonymity. Reports can be submitted electronically or mailed.

- If you file a NASA report after an incident or occurrence, the FAA considers you to have a "constructive attitude". This most likely means that you'll try to prevent further violations. Although a finding of violation may be made, **neither a civil penalty nor certificate suspension will be imposed if:**

  - the violation was inadvertent and not deliberate;
  - the violation did not involve a criminal offense, or accident, or action under 49 U.S.C. Section 44709 which discloses a lack of qualification or competency, which is wholly excluded from this policy;
  - the person has not been found in any prior FAA enforcement action to have committed a violation of 49 U.S.C. Subtitle VII, or any regulation promulgated there **for a period of 5 years prior** to the date of occurrence; and
  - the person proves that, **within 10 days after the violation**, he or she completed and delivered or mailed a written report of the incident or occurrence to NASA under **ASRS.**

YOU and ATC

Radio Frequencies

Emergency Frequency – 121.5
This is monitored by Flight Service, civilian and military control towers, approach controls, and centers.

MULTICOM – 122.9
Used at airports without an operating control tower, Flight Service or UNICOM (122.8).

Local Airport Advisory Service
Flight Service will provide this service when they are located at an airport that doesn't have a control tower, or when the control tower is not in service. The Common Traffic Advisory Frequency (CTAF) at an uncontrolled airport is usually 123.6.

Getting Along With ATC

Initial call, use your model instead of make – "Cherokee 7482J". This helps ATC understand your performance capability.

Use your full call sign until the controller calls you by the shortened call sign.

ATC sizes up pilots and their abilities as soon as they check in on frequency. If you are clear, concise, and use proper phraseology, this gives controllers confidence that you'll understand and do a good job when given ATC instructions. *Here's some phraseology that will send you directly to the penalty box:*

- Saying things like "sugar" (instead of "sierra") "nickel" (instead of "fife"), or "pop" (instead of "papa").
- Starting a transmission with, "and" or "ahh." If you're not ready to talk, don't press the button. Try not to sound distracted and bumbling.
- Initiating a call to ATC by saying, ". . . with you." It wastes radio time. Beside, the controller knows that you're "with" him or her!
- "Tally ho." It's not a fox hunt! "Negative contact", or "Traffic in sight", is fine.
- "I've got 'em on the fish finder." If you have a traffic alert

system in your aircraft, that phrase doesn't help ATC and you sound like you're at your favorite fishin' hole.
- ○ Aviation slang or CB lingo. Leave it in the truck.
- ○ "Roger" means I've received your transmission. It doesn't me yes, no, or I'll do it.

Check in Like a Pro
- ○ **Departure Control** — First call, report the <u>altitude you're passing</u> and the <u>altitude assigned</u>.
- ○ **Center** — First call, report the altitude you're passing and the altitude assigned.
- ○ There are only three ways to report an altitude: "CLIMBING", "DESCENDING", and "LEVEL." Never use decimals, like "2.6" for 2,600 feet.
- ○ **The Approach Controller** — Always check-in with the ATIS letter.
- ○ **The Tower Controller** — If VFR, give tower your bearing and distance from the airport, plus the ATIS letter. Never say, ". . . with the numbers."

At Uncontrolled Airports
- ○ "Taking the active" or "clearing the active" confuses inbound pilots. The runway has a name, so use it.

Don't Make Controllers Wonder, "Which frequency is that guy on?"
- ○ If you're in the run-up area, stay on Ground Control. Switch to Tower when you're ready to depart.
- ○ After landing, don't switch to *Ground* control unless you've cleared the runway's hold short line <u>and</u> Tower has told you to switch to Ground. Any questions, ask.

AOPA's online course, *"Say it Right"*, is available at AOPA.org

MOUNTAIN FLYING

Travel Tips

- Approach a ridge line on a 45° angle and depart it on a 90° angle. If you encounter a dangerous downdraft, and you're on a 45, instead of turning 180 degrees, you'll only need to turn 45 degrees to become parallel to the ridge, and on your way to safety.
- Mountain winds greater than 20 knots: Fasten your seat belt.
- Mountain winds greater than 30 knots: Consider flying another day.
- Density Altitude INCREASES when temperatures INCREASE and altimeter settings DECREASE.

Lenticular Clouds are just like mountains. They come in different shapes and sizes. Lens shaped clouds form on the lee side (downwind) of the mountains. As the air is forced upward, it cools enough for water vapor to condense. While the cloud appears stationary, the winds can be impressive.

Cap Clouds are similar to Lenticular Clouds. They form directly over a mountain, (mostly on the windward side), as humid air is forced to flow over the mountain, condensing into a cloud. Although appearing motionless, the wind is anything but stationary.

Wave Clouds form on the lee side (downwind) of the ridge line. The corkscrew appearance is attributed to the wave pattern being nearly parallel with the upper level airflow.

Kelvin-Helmholtz Cloud waves form on the lee side of mountains. Expect a strong vertical sheer.

*Airspeed, altitude and brains:
Two of them are always needed to successfully complete the flight.*

Mountain Waves

When the air meets the mountain on the windward side, it's fairly smooth. As it "climbs" the mountain, lifting develops and the wind speed increases, reaching its maximum speed at the summit. As it passes the crest, the flow becomes more complicated, with lots of downdrafts.

Further downwind, some five to ten miles from the summit, the airflow begins to climb in a definite wave pattern. Additional waves, generally less intense than the primary wave, may also develop downwind.

Depending on the wind speed and the atmosphere's stability, the distance between following waves can be from two to ten miles. Wave lengths up to 20 miles have been reported.

Sometimes, (not always), you can look at the clouds, and predict mountain waves.

Smooth clouds generally have smoother airflow, and with light turbulence. Clouds appearing ragged or irregular indicate more turbulence.

WARNING: it is possible for wave action to take place when the air is too dry to form clouds. This makes identifying and forecasting mountain waves more difficult.

AOPA's online course, "*Mountain Flying*", is available at AOPA.org

"There's a big difference between a pilot and an aviator.
One is a technician. The other is an artist in love with flight." — Captain Elrey Jeppesen

WINTER FLYING

Preflight. Ensure that you check the lights and pitot heat; ports, static ports, oil breather, stall warning horn, etc.

Ice can melt in the control surface hinges and re-freeze. Ensure that antennas, probes, and access doors are firmly attached. Make sure the top of each wing and tail is free of ice, both visually and by touch. Clear ice can be very hard to see, but a tactile inspection with a flashlight can find it.

All the Snow & Ice Must Go

Don't expect loose snow to blow off. The smallest amount of frost on an airfoil slows the air flow and can prevent an aircraft from becoming airborne. Even if you manage to make it off the ground, your aircraft could stall in the climb.

Preheating (Below 32°F)

Warm batteries just crank better, and instruments are happier when they're warm. Forced air heat can have an amazing effect on your instruments and engine start.

NOTE: If you run the battery down in freezing temps, be sure to charge it immediately.

Taxiing in Slush and Ice? Taxi slow. If slush is sprayed onto your gear, you can bet that it will freeze solid at altitude. If you have retractable gear, you might have a problem getting the gear down when you land.

Water in the Fuel Supply can freeze and block fuel lines, so keep fuel tanks full to prevent water condensation.
Change your fuel cap seals every year, and lubricate them often to keep them pliable. Make sure that the fuel selector operates smoothly.

When Starting you'll need more fuel in the fuel/air mixture.
Add at least one more priming stroke than you would on a warm day.
Observe the starter's limitations. Don't overwork it. Check oil pressure after engine start.
*To prevent spark plug fouling, do not idle lower than 1,000 RPM and lean your engine as much as possible.
During the run-up, make sure you're not slipping and skidding.

Switch Tanks every 30 minutes. If the fuel selector freezes, you'll still have fuel to find an airport.

Exercise the Propeller when you switch tanks. This helps prevent congealing hub oil.

Carbon Monoxide is a Big Concern in the Winter. . If you detect the odor of exhaust or feel drowsy, dizzy, or have a headache while using the heater, you should suspect carbon monoxide poisoning.

High Oil Temps are Great! The higher the better, because this helps vaporize the moisture.

AOPA's online course, "Weather Wise: Precipitation & Icing", is available at AOPA.org

Airport Watch

The Airport Watch Program was developed by the Airport Owners and Pilots Association (AOPA) and the Transportation Security Administration (TSA).

Lock Up — Secure Your Airplane

- Lock your aircraft doors and consider locks for the prop(s), throttle(s), and wheels.
- Always lock hangar doors, even if you're just going for a short trip around the pattern.
- Keep your ignition keys separate from the aircraft.

Look Out — Secure Your Airport. *Watch Out for:*

- Anyone trying to access an aircraft through force—without keys, using a crowbar or screwdriver.
- Anyone unfamiliar with aviation procedures trying to check out an aircraft.
- Anyone who misuses aviation lingo—or seems too eager to use all the lingo.
- People or groups determined to keep to themselves.
- Anyone who appears to be just loitering, with no specific reason for being there.
- Out-of-the-ordinary videotaping of aircraft or hangars
- Dangerous cargo or loads—explosives, chemicals, openly displayed weapons—being loaded into an aircraft.
- Anything that strikes you as wrong—listen to your gut instinct, and then follow through
- Pay special attention to height, weight, and the individual's clothing or other identifiable traits.

You're not trained in police matters! You should never approach someone you fear may be about to commit an illegal act or crime. Make some notes, such as the person's appearance, clothing, car license plate, type of aircraft, N number, and coloring. If appropriate, take a picture, but keep your distance if the situation seems hostile.

If you can't safely contact authorities or the airport management without exposing yourself to risk, leave the field or go to your car and talk on your cell phone. It could be your best weapon in fighting airport crime.

Report suspicious activity to 866/GA-SECURE

AOPA's online course, "*General Aviation Security*", is available at AOPA.org

Other books by James D Price

Track Expenses will help you keep
perfect records. You can record
aircraft squawks, and keep track of
maintenance and oil changes.
There's even a spot to record VOR
checks and GPS data updates each
month.

With **Track Expenses Like a PRO,**
you'll always know when inspections
are due, how much your aircraft
costs per year, and you'll be ready
for taxes with business and
charitable deductions.

**Track Expenses
Like a PRO**

Aircraft Owner's Expense and
Maintenance Tracking System
Single or Multi Engine

Keep perfect records.
Know when inspections are due,
what your aircraft costs per year, and
document business and charitable deductions.

James D Price, ATP, CFII/MEI
Retired Airline Captain, Col. USAFR (Ret)

ISBN 9780977723546

For more information, visit Jim's website at:

http://www.JDPriceCFI.com

Printed in the U.S.A.
http://www.WritersCramp.us

CPSIA information can be obtained at www.ICGtesting.com
Printed in the USA
266613BV00005B/1/P